KT-442-363

the complete
gluten-free baker

more than 80 *deliciously gluten-free recipes*

Hannah Miles

photography by William Reavell

rps

RYLAND PETERS & SMALL
LONDON • NEW YORK

Dedication
For Lucy and David, with love x

Designers Megan Smith, Iona Hoyle
and Paul Stradling
Editors Julia Charles and Rebecca Woods
Production Gordana Simakovic, Patricia
Harrington and David Hearn
Editorial Director Julia Charles
Art Director Leslie Harrington
Publisher Cindy Richards

Prop Stylists Liz Belton and Lisa Harrison
Food Stylists Joss Herd, Bridget Sargeson
and Jack Sargeson
Indexer Hilary Bird

First published in 2016 by
Ryland Peters & Small
20–21 Jockey's Fields
London WC1R 4BW
and
341 East 116th Street
New York NY 10019
www.rylandpeters.com

Printed and bound in China

10 9 8 7 6 5 4 3 2 1

Text © Hannah Miles 2011, 2013, 2016
Design and photographs © Ryland Peters
& Small 2011

NOTE: The recipes in this book have been
previously published in two separate
volumes, **The Gluten-free Baker** and
The Savoury Gluten-free Baker.

ISBN: 978-1-84975-762-1

All rights reserved. No part of this publication
may be reproduced, stored in a retrieval system
or transmitted in any form or by any means,
electronic, mechanical, photocopying or
otherwise, without the prior permission of
the publisher.

A CIP record for this book is available from
the British Library.
US Library of Congress cataloguing-in-
publication data has been applied for.

Author's acknowledgements
A huge thank you to Ryland Peters & Small for
publishing this compendium of my gluten-free
books, a wonderful collection of my favourite
recipes. Special thanks to Julia Charles for
commissioning the book, a dear friend who
I love to spend time with sipping cocktails and
chatting all things cooking; Megan Smith, Iona
Hoyle and Paul Stradling for their beautiful design
and to Leslie Harrington for perfect art direction;
Joss Herd, Bridget Sargeson and Jack Sargeson
for their gorgeous food styling; and to William
Reavell for his stunning photography. Special
thanks too to my agent Heather of HHB Agency
for all the years of support. Much love to all my
friends and family who tasted recipe after recipe
and to David, Christine, Lucy, Jennifer, Maren, Elka
and Susan for their kind recipe contributions. And
special thanks to my best friend Lucy Deakin, the
inspiration for this book – may your days always
be filled with delicious gluten free cake. Finally,
a very special thank you goes to Amy Peterson of
Coeliac UK for her help and guidance – Coeliac
UK is a leading charity working for people living
with coeliac disease and dermatitis herpetiformis.
Visit them at www.coeliac.org.uk or call the
Helpline on 0845 305 2060 for information and
support. In the US visit www.celiac.org or www.
celiac.com for information, advice and support.

contents

introduction

This book aims to provide delicious alternatives to favourite recipes that people suffering from coeliac disease or gluten intolerance miss the most – pastries, cakes, breads and comforting oven bakes – simple home baking that, when you are first diagnosed, seems an impossibility. With a little know-how and some simple ingredients, this book will return you to baking.

When developing these recipes, I read a lot of books on gluten-free cooking. These seemed to require endless combining of different flours and a lengthy list of non-storecupboard ingredients. There seemed to be no clear explanation of which flour to use when and in what quantities. All in all it was very intimidating, even for someone who bakes as much as I do. What I wanted were some good basic recipes that used ingredients that I was familiar with – gluten-free flours, ground nuts, polenta, desiccated coconut and such like. Ready-combined flours seemed the simplest solution and avoided the need for combining many different types of gluten-free flour – such as tapioca, potato and rice – as they have already been combined by the manufacturers in what I imagine must be the best possible combination following rigorous testing. Using these ready-blended flours lets you bake as you would with regular flour and achieve excellent results. Keep two or three bags in the kitchen storecupboard and you can bake perfect gluten-free cakes, breads and pastry whenever needed. It is then just a question of understanding the characteristics of the particular gluten-free flours you are using, and adding other ingredients to provide the extra moisture needed and of course plenty of flavour.

The aim of this book is therefore simple: to make things that taste so good that you would never know they were gluten-free. You can serve these recipes to the whole family and all of your friends and no one will notice the difference.

What is Coeliac/Celiac Disease?

Coeliac disease is an auto-immune disease, which affect the intestines, leading to poor absorption of gluten. Symptoms of the disease can leave those affected feeling very unwell and lacking in energy, as well as having an upset stomach and other symptoms. There is currently no cure for the condition but it can be managed well with a change in diet.

It is important that medical advice is taken by anyone who feels they might be experiencing a sensitivity to gluten, to ascertain whether they are a coeliac or are experiencing an allergic reaction to gluten and/or wheat. Each person's symptoms are unique – some people will be able to eat some ingredients that cause problems for others. Testing is available and it is important to take steps to understand what is suitable for you to eat. It can be a steep learning curve but within a few months you will learn which brands of chocolate, poppadoms, stock cubes and so on don't contain gluten and are safe for you to enjoy.

Sometimes coeliac disease is also coupled with other allergies and you may find that some other products, which are gluten-free, also make you unwell. With time and experience you will have a clear understanding of your own limitations.

Gluten is present in varying levels in wheat, barley and rye cereals and also sometimes in oats, although this is thought most likely caused by cross-contamination with other cereals during processing. Some people sensitive to gluten can eat oats and oat flour (see page 10) and as these are a good staple ingredient in baking, some of the recipes in this book use them. but always make sure that you buy brands labelled 'gluten-free' to be safe. You should always check, however, whether the person you are baking for is intolerant to oats.

Managing a Gluten-free Diet

Whilst it is easy to avoid products that very obviously contain wheat and gluten – bread, cakes, pasta – there are a variety of products that contain traces of gluten, some of which are not obvious. It is not always easy to avoid such pitfalls and it is therefore essential to carefully check the ingredients list on product packaging or refer to the manufacturer to ensure that products are gluten-free. At the outset of a gluten-free diet you may find it helps to keep a food diary to record what you eat as this can help to identify problem foods that have made you ill. Some brands of a type of product may be gluten-free whereas others may not – very careful reading of ingredients labels is always essential. Nowadays many products are labelled as 'gluten-free', which makes life much easier.

All forms of wheat, barley, rye and spelt must be avoided. This means that regular flours and breads are out, as well as wheat-based products, such as beer and pasta. Gluten is commonly used by food manufacturers in a wide variety of food preparation and can be found in ready-meals and pre-produced food. A small trace of wheat used as a thickener in a sauce may make you really unwell but checking the label will help you to spot unsafe ingredients. Products that are coated in breadcrumbs are also not suitable for people with gluten intolerance.

You need to be extra vigilant at all stages of cooking. It is so easy to take a packet from the kitchen cupboard and add to a recipe without checking whether the item contains gluten – I have found myself doing this on occasion and have just stopped myself in time. I once made stock from chicken bones of a roast chicken, but the chicken had contained a breadcrumb stuffing so there was a good chance that the stock was contaminated with gluten. Luckily I remembered in time before serving to my friend who is a coeliac. With time and practice you will become familiar with which ingredients are safe and which are not.

The best advice is just to take a bit of time before you start cooking. Assemble all of your ingredients and check that they are all safe to use before starting to cook. Some of the less obvious products that contain gluten include the following:

Anti-caking agents – these are used to prevent the clumping and sticking together of ingredients during food production and can contain traces of wheat. They are found in some icing/confectioners' sugars, dried fruits and coconut so check labels carefully. Powdered fondant icing sugar and unrefined icing/confectioners' sugar do not generally contain an anti-caking agent and can be used to make glacé, royal and butter icings/frostings. When selecting dried fruit, choose brands that are separated using a light coating of oil rather than an anti-caking agent. Happily, maize, tapioca and potato-starch based anti-caking agents are also now commonly being used by manufacturers so this is becoming less of an issue.

Yeast – some dried yeasts contain wheat as a bulking agent. For safe gluten-free baking, use either fresh yeast or a gluten-free dried yeast, both of which are stocked by most supermarkets and health food shops.

Baking powder – some baking powders contain wheat. Many manufacturers are now using rice flour in place of wheat flour and so gluten-free baking powder is now more commonly available in supermarkets.

Dried milk powder/non-fat dry milk – ice cream and chocolate can contain milk powders/non-fat dry milk bulked out with wheat. In addition, some coeliacs cannot tolerate white or milk chocolate because lactose intolerance is associated with the disease, although it is a temporary condition in the majority of people that rectifies itself after a person adopts a gluten-free diet.

Malt products – malted drinks should all be avoided as they are wheat based, but malt extract can usually be tolerated in small amounts, e.g. in breakfast cereals. Malt vinegar is suitable as the protein is removed in the processing.

Soy sauce and Worcestershire sauce – these also contain gluten so look out for gluten-free brands.

Processed meat products – products such as sausages, salamis and pâtés can contain wheat as rusk is a common ingredient so always read the labels carefully.

Sauces, gravy powders, stocks (cubes and liquid) and powdered spices – these can sometimes be bulked out with wheat products so again always check the labels.

Instant coffees – some contain wheat as a bulking agent. Fresh ground coffee, which can be used to make espresso or filter coffee in a machine, can be used instead as this generally does not contain any gluten.

Glacé cherries – these can contain gluten. Use fresh cherries or preserved cherries as a good substitute in baking – in my opinion, they always taste nicer anyway!

Sour cream – some processes for making sour cream use wheat so it is important to use a brand that is 'pure' and gluten-free. Checking the manufacturers' website will assist with this.

The above list is not exhaustive but should give you a good idea of just how rigorous you have to be with product checking.

Gluten-free Baking

The key to successful gluten-free baking is to understand the ingredients and their properties. Gluten gives elasticity to the doughs from which breads and cakes are made. Gluten-free substitutes lack this elasticity and need to be handled slightly differently. The one good thing is that as the doughs are not elastic, bread doughs need no kneading, sparing your arm muscles somewhat! Generally speaking, gluten-free doughs and mixes require a lot more liquid than wheat-based recipes and if there is not enough liquid the items will have a powdery texture and crumble when you cut them. Adding natural yogurt, buttermilk or sour cream to cake mixtures will result in moist cakes. Pastry can be very crumbly without the elasticity of gluten and must be very carefully worked. Adding cheese to savoury pastry or cream cheese to sweet pastry can help bind the dough together. Rather than rolling the pastry out into large sheets that are likely to crumble when lifted, the best method for lining a pastry case is to gently press in small pieces of the pastry dough into the tin/pan until it is lined entirely with a thin layer of pastry.

Some gluten-free flours have a slightly bitter taste that can spoil the flavour of baked goods. The best way to mask this is to ensure each recipe is packed full of flavour.

The Gluten-free Baking Pantry

For successful baking you need to equip yourself with a few basic ingredients. Once you have developed confidence from following these recipes, you can then experiment with other recipes. Below is a list of essential ingredients you will need for the recipes in this book.

Gluten-free blended flours – there is now a wide variety of gluten-free flours available in supermarkets and wholefood stores and these are the easiest flours to start with. They are ready mixed and are specifically designed to give the best results. In the UK three types are available – plain flour for cookies and pastry, self-raising flour for cakes and some breads, and strong white flour for breads and some pastries. In the US all-purpose flour is available but I've yet to find a self-raising/rising one so have tested

the recipes in this book with Bob's Red Mill gluten-free all-purpose baking flour, adding gluten-free baking powder and xanthan gum, which gives a very good result. Whilst you can combine your own mixes of rice, potato and cornflour/cornstarch, it is more convenient to use these ready-mixed flours.

Buckwheat flour – contrary to its name, buckwheat does not contain any wheat – it is made from the seeds of a flowering plant that is associated with the rhubarb family. The seeds resemble beechnuts and it is a common misunderstanding that this flour is made from beechnuts. The flour has a strong taste, which can be overpowering and slightly medicinal if used in large quantities, but it is ideal for pancakes and blinis and can be used in some cakes. (Be aware that a very small number of people experience an allergic reaction to buckwheat so it's essential to check with the person you are baking for.)

Chestnut flour – this is made from ground sweet chestnuts and has a delicious smoky flavour. Due to this smokiness, it is only really suitable for savoury recipes.

Gram flour – this is made from ground chickpeas and is often used in Indian dishes, such as pakora and bhajis and also various flatbreads. Most poppadoms are made with gram flour but it is important to check that it has not been combined with wheat flour. Italian *farina di ceci* is a similar product and can be substituted.

Coconut flour – this is made from dried coconut flesh, which has been ground to a fine powder. You can make your own by grinding desiccated coconut to a fine powder in a food processor and then sifting it, although if your desiccated coconut is sweetened you will need to reduce the sugar in the recipe and check that the desiccated coconut does not contain any wheat as an anti-caking agent or coating (for more information see page 7).

Cornflour/cornstarch – this is made from finely ground grains of corn. It is an excellent thickener and can be used in sauces.

Polenta/cornmeal – this is a useful staple of gluten-free baking. Coarse grains can be cooked in water to a thick paste and added to cakes and breads to give a golden colour, moist texture and rich flavour. Fine meal is more like flour in texture and can be used in breads and muffins.

Almond meal and ground almonds – almond meal is a coarse ground flour which contains the skin of the whole almonds. It is therefore darker in texture than ground almonds and is ideal in cookies and cakes. Ground almonds are one of the most common ingredients in this book as they make cakes very moist and do not have a strong flavour so can carry other flavours well. You can make you own ground almonds or almond meal by blitzing whole or skinned almonds in a food processor. When buying ready ground almonds check the ingredients as some cheap varieties include breadcrumbs as a bulking agent (and therefore gluten).

Nuts – a lot of the recipes in this book use other ground nuts, such as pecans, walnuts and hazelnuts. They are an ideal replacement for flour – they create a moist texture and add delicious flavour. If you do not have the nut called for in the recipe you can generally substitute another nut in its place. By grinding the nuts in a food processor until very fine then combining them with a small amount of gluten-free flour they make a good substitute.

Oats – not all people who are intolerant to gluten are able to eat oats. The protein in oats is similar to gluten and so can also be an issue for some coeliacs, although it may cause different symptoms. If in any doubt do not use them. However, there are some people who are intolerant to gluten who are able to eat oats – make sure you choose brands labelled gluten-free to be safe.

Oat flour – this is made from finely ground oats. As stated above, some oats contains traces of gluten so it is important to ensure that the oat flour you use is gluten free and that the person you are cooking for can eat oats, Oat flour is available from health food shops and online.

Quinoa flour – this flour is made from ground quinoa grains which are gluten free, nutritious and have a great texture. It is particularly good for making pasta. It has quite a strong, slightly medicinal smell and I therefore always use it combined with other flours.

Ondwha flour – this is an Indian flour made from ground rice and lentils and is available in Indian supermarkets and online. If you are not able to find this flour, there are online recipes explaining how to make the flour at home yourself.

Gluten-free baking powder – this is an essential raising/rising agent and is used to make cakes and breads rise during baking.

Xanthan gum – this is used in gluten-free baking to bind, thicken and stabilize ingredients and is ideal for use in doughs, pastry and breads. It's made by fermenting corn sugar with a microbial bacteria and is used extensively in the food industry.

Dairy ingredients – these are essential for moist, non-crumbly cakes – in this book the recipes use buttermilk, plain yogurt and sour cream. Again, it is essential to check the product labels as some creams may contain traces of gluten. If you prefer, you can make your own sour cream by adding the juice of a lemon to 300 ml/1¼ cups double/heavy cream. If you do not have the liquid ingredient called for in the recipe you can easily substitute

– for example if you do not have buttermilk available, mix together half milk and half plain yogurt to the same quantity of buttermilk. The results will be equally delicious.

Butter and fats – some margarines may contain gluten so it is best to use good-quality unsalted butter in all recipes to remain gluten-free.

Eggs – eggs do not contain gluten and are used in most of the recipes in this book. By separating the eggs and whisking the egg whites separately and folding into a cake batter, you can add additional air to your cakes, making them light and delicious.

Extra virgin coconut oil – this is usually sold in jars in a set form and adds a delicious coconut flavour to recipes.

Flavouring agents – vanilla and almond extracts are ideal for masking the sometimes mildly unpleasant 'flavour' of gluten-free flours. Always check the labelling to ensure that flavourings are gluten-free.

Syrups and honeys – pure maple syrup, golden/light corn syrup, treacle and honey are all gluten-free and are delicious sweeteners in baking recipes.

Alcohols – this can be a confusing area for those who are gluten-intolerant. Beer is made with hops and so must be avoided. Some brands of whiskey (and Irish cream liqueurs) may contain gluten from the caramel colouring which is added, although pure whiskey does not contain gluten. Before using any alcohol, it's wise to check the full ingredients on the manufacturer's website.

Avoiding Contamination
One key requirement of successful gluten-free baking is to avoid cross-contamination. If you have a member of the family who is intolerant to gluten, the best solution is to remove all products containing gluten from the house. Whilst this is the most effective way to avoid the risk of cross contamination, I recognize that this is not always practical. Where total removal is not possible, the best advice is to keep gluten-free products in sealed containers in a separate place away from products containing gluten. Label everything clearly so that there can be no confusion.

10

If you have been baking with regular flour, small particles released into the air during cooking can land on cooking equipment, work surfaces and kitchen towels and leave traces of gluten. It is therefore important to wipe down all equipment, appliances, surfaces and utensils thoroughly and use clean cloths and aprons. It takes a surprisingly small amount of exposure to gluten to make someone ill.

Cross-contamination is also possible through using kitchen equipment, such as toasters, baking sheets and wire racks. Silicone sleeves (Toastabags) can be used to shield toasters from gluten contamination or, if possible, have a separate toaster and other similar appliances just for gluten-free products. Also consider investing in some silicon mats that you can set aside just for gluten-free baking. It is also important to avoid putting knives and spoons that have been exposed to gluten into butters, spreads and jams/jellies as these can also cause contamination. If it is practical, have separate tubs and jars clearly labelled as 'gluten-free'. Where possible, store these away from products that may contain traces of gluten.

Where to Go for Advice

If you believe that you may have a gluten intolerance or coeliac disease, it is essential to seek professional medical advice. Once you have been diagnosed with either, there are many sources of information available to you. The Coeliac Societies in the UK and USA are able to provide a large amount of advice and support (see page 4). Local support groups can also offer guidance on managing day-to-day life without gluten. In addition, there are a wide variety of books on this subject and some fantastic resources are available online offering a wealth of information. Particularly useful are the forums where coeliacs can communicate with each other and share advice on all aspects of living and enjoying a gluten-free lifestyle.

cookies, brownies & bars

These giant chocolate chip cookies will put a smile on everyone's face. Delicious with a glass of ice-cold milk, packed full of dark and white chocolate, they are a perfect home-coming treat. It is important that the chocolate you use does not contain skimmed milk powder as this can contains gluten so check the labels carefully. Gluten-free white chocolate buttons are available in most larger supermarkets.

chocolate chip cookies

Preheat the oven to 180°C (350°F) Gas 4.

Put the butter and both sugars in a mixing bowl and cream together. Add the flour, bicarbonate of soda/baking soda, ground almonds, egg and buttermilk and whisk well until everything is incorporated. Mix in the dark chocolate and white chocolate buttons with a wooden spoon.

Put 20 tablespoonfuls of the mixture on the prepared baking sheets, leaving a gap between each one as the cookies will spread during baking. (You may need to bake in batches depending on the size of your baking sheets.)

Bake in the preheated oven for about 10–12 minutes, until the cookies are golden brown. Leave to cool on the baking sheets for a few minutes then transfer to a wire rack to cool completely.

These cookies will keep for up to 5 days if stored in an airtight container.

125 g/1 stick plus 1 tablespoon unsalted butter, softened

125 g/⅔ cup caster/granulated sugar

125 g/½ cup dark soft brown sugar

150 g/1 cup plus 2 tablespoons gluten-free plain/all-purpose baking flour

1 teaspoon bicarbonate of soda/ baking soda

100 g/1 cup ground almonds

1 egg, beaten

60 ml/¼ cup buttermilk

100 g/3½ oz dark chocolate, chopped

100 g/3½ oz white chocolate buttons

2 baking sheets, greased and lined

Makes about 20 cookies

These oat and coconut cookies are delicious and have a crisp buttery texture – perfect for an afternoon teatime treat. I prefer to make these cookies whilst the mixture is still warm from heating the syrup as this causes the cookies to spread out thinly and gives a crisp buttery texture. If you prefer a chewier cookie, let the mixture go cold and place mounds of the dough on the baking sheet, as the cookies will spread out less this way. Please bear in mind that not all people with gluten or wheat intolerance can eat oats but gluten-free oats are now available so these are best to use.

oat & coconut cookies

150 g/1 stick plus 2 tablespoons butter

3 generous tablespoons golden/light corn syrup

170 g/1 cup gluten-free porridge/rolled oats

85 g/1 generous cup long soft shredded coconut

60 g/1 scant cup flaked coconut

115 g/½ cup plus 1 tablespoon caster/granulated sugar

115 g gluten-free self-raising flour OR 1 scant cup gluten-free all-purpose baking flour plus 1 teaspoon baking powder and ¼ teaspoon xanthan gum

2 baking sheets, greased and lined

Makes about 24 cookies

Preheat the oven to 180°C (350°F) Gas 4.

Put the butter and syrup in a small saucepan and melt over gentle heat. Put the oats, both coconuts, sugar and flour in a mixing bowl. Pour the melted butter mixture over the dry ingredients and mix well with a wooden spoon, until everything is incorporated.

Put 24 tablespoonfuls of the mixture on the prepared baking sheets, a distance apart as they will spread during baking. (You may need to bake in batches depending on the size of your baking sheets.)

Bake in the preheated oven for 10–15 minutes, until the cookies are golden brown. Watch closely towards the end of cooking as they can turn brown very quickly. Leave to cool on the baking sheets.

These cookies will keep for up to 5 days if stored in an airtight container.

Ginger cookies are perfect on a cold day. Warming pieces of ginger and tangy lime always soothe away life's troubles. If you prefer, you can replace the lime zest with orange zest and a pinch of cinnamon for a more festive feel. These cookies store well in an airtight tin and can be frozen on the day they are made.

ginger cookies

Preheat the oven to 180°C (350°F) Gas 4.

Put the flour, bicarbonate of soda/baking soda, ground almonds, caster sugar, ground ginger and lime zest in a mixing bowl and mix together. Put the butter and ginger syrup in a small saucepan and heat gently until the butter has melted. Let cool slightly and then stir into the dry ingredients, along with the chopped ginger. Put about 18 tablespoonfuls of the mixture on the prepared baking sheets, leaving a gap between each as the cookies will spread during cooking. (You may need to bake in batches depending on the size of your baking sheets.)

Bake in the preheated oven for about 12–15 minutes, until the cookies are golden brown. Leave to cool on the baking sheets for a few minutes then transfer to a wire rack with a spatula to cool.

These cookies will keep for up to 5 days if stored in an airtight container.

160 g gluten-free self-raising flour OR 1⅓ cups gluten-free all-purpose baking flour plus 1½ teaspoons baking powder and ¾ teaspoon xanthan gum

1 teaspoon bicarbonate of soda/ baking soda

180 g/2 cups ground almonds

180 g/1 cup caster/granulated sugar

2 teaspoons ground ginger

finely grated zest of 2 limes

125 g/1 stick plus 1 tablespoon butter

6 pieces of stem ginger in syrup, finely chopped plus 3 tablespoons ginger syrup from the jar

2 baking sheets, greased and lined

Makes about 18 cookies

These cookies smell truly delicious as you remove them from the oven.
Do use culinary lavender, which has not been sprayed with pesticides.

lavender shortbreads

115 g/1 stick butter, softened

60 g/⅓ cup caster/superfine or
granulated sugar,

85 g/⅔ cup gluten-free plain/
all-purpose baking flour

2 teaspoons culinary lavender,
finely ground

85 g/¾ cup ground almonds

a little milk, if required

almond meal flour, for rolling out

2 baking sheets, greased and lined

Makes 20 shortbreads

Preheat the oven to 180°C (350°F) Gas 4.

Put the butter and sugar in a mixing bowl and cream together until light and creamy. Sift in the flour and add the lavender and ground almonds. Bring together to a dough with your hands. If the mixture is too dry add a little milk to moisten it.

Transfer the dough to a work surface. Roll the dough into a long sausage shape, 5-cm/2-in diameter. Roll in almond meal flour so that it coats the edge of the dough. Chill in the fridge for 30 minutes. Cut into 1-cm/1⁄2-inch thick slices and arrange on the prepared baking sheets a small distance apart. Press the back of a fork down into each shortbread to make ridges.

Bake in the preheated oven for 12–15 minutes, until golden brown. Remove from the oven. Let cool on the baking sheets before serving.

These shortbreads will keep for up to 5 days if stored in an airtight container.

Caramel or millionaire's shortbread is always popular – a buttery cookie base with a layer of rich, gooey caramel topped with milk/semisweet chocolate. You can replace the milk chocolate topping with dark or white gluten-free chocolate if you prefer and decorate with gluten-free sprinkles for a pretty party effect.

caramel shortbread

Preheat the oven to 180°C (350°F) Gas 4.

To make the shortbread base, put the butter and sugar in a mixing bowl and cream together. Sift in the flour then add the almonds and bring the mixture together with your hands to form a soft dough. Press into the prepared tin/pan and prick all over with a fork. Bake in the preheated oven for 15–20 minutes, until the shortbread is golden brown. Let cool in the tin/pan.

Put the sugar, butter, condensed milk and vanilla extract in a small saucepan and warm over gentle heat until the butter has melted and the sugar dissolved. Bring to the boil, beating all the time so that the mixture doesn't stick, then reduce the heat and simmer for about 5 minutes, until golden brown and thick. Pour over the shortbread base and let cool.

To make the chocolate topping, put the chocolate in a heatproof bowl set over a saucepan of barely simmering water and stir gently until melted. Pour the chocolate over the caramel and leave to set. Use a hot knife to cut into 16 squares to serve.

These shortbreads will keep for up to 5 days if stored in an airtight container.

For the shortbread base
115 g/1 stick butter, softened
60 g/⅓ cup caster/granulated sugar
85 g gluten-free self-raising flour OR ¾ cup gluten-free all-purpose baking flour plus 1 teaspoon baking powder and ⅛ teaspoon xanthan gum
85 g/1 cup ground almonds

For the caramel layer
60 g/⅓ cup caster/granulated sugar
60 g/½ stick butter
300 g/1 cup condensed milk
1 teaspoon vanilla extract
For the chocolate topping
150 g/5½ oz milk/semisweet chocolate

For the topping
150 g/5½ oz milk/semisweet chocolate

a 20-cm/8-inch square baking tin/pan, greased and lined (base and sides)

Makes 16 shortbreads

These are moist, crumbly brownies that quite literally melt in the mouth. Walnuts are ground finely and used in place of flour, which is what gives the brownies such a wonderfully nutty flavour.

white chocolate & walnut brownies

250 g/2 sticks plus 2 tablespoons butter

300 g/10½ oz dark chocolate (70% cocoa solids)

300 g/1½ cups plus 1 tablespoon caster/granulated sugar

200 g/1½ cups dark soft brown sugar

5 large eggs

1 teaspoon vanilla extract

100 g gluten-free self-raising flour OR generous ¾ cup gluten-free all-purpose baking flour plus 1 teaspoon baking powder and ½ teaspoon xanthan gum

200 g/2 cups shelled walnuts, finely ground

150 g/1 cup white chocolate buttons

a 33 x 23-cm/13 x 9-inch baking tin/pan, greased and base-lined

Makes 20 brownies

Preheat the oven to 190°C (375°F) Gas 5.

Melt the butter and dark chocolate in a heatproof bowl set over a pan of simmering water or in a microwave proof bowl in the microwave on high power for 1 minute and stir to ensure there are no lumps. Set aside to cool.

Whisk the caster/granulated sugar and dark brown sugar with the eggs and vanilla extract until the mixture is very light and has doubled in size. Whilst still whisking, slowly pour in the melted chocolate and butter mixture. Fold in the flour and ground walnuts, then pour the mixture into the prepared tin/pan. Sprinkle over the chocolate buttons (which should sink into the mixture) ensuring that they are evenly distributed.

Bake in the preheated oven for about 30–40 minutes, until the brownies have formed a crust and a knife inserted into the middle of the tin/pan comes out clean with no cake batter on it. Allow to cool before cutting into squares.

These brownies will keep for up to 5 days if stored in an airtight container.

Two delicious teatime treats – the flapjack and the brownie – are combined in this tempting recipe. The base is packed with coconut and pecans and the brownie rich with dark chocolate. If you are not able to find hazelnut flour, you can substitute gluten-free plain/all-purpose baking flour.

flapjack pecan brownies

Preheat the oven to 190°C (375°F) Gas 5.

To make the flapjack base, put the butter in a saucepan and melt over low heat. Stir in the sugar, coconut and pecans. Mix well so that everything is coated in butter and sugar. Spoon the mixture into the prepared tin/pan and press down evenly with the back of a spoon.

To make the brownie topping, melt the butter and chocolate in a heatproof bowl set over a pan of simmering water. Remove the bowl from the heat and set aside to cool. Put both the sugars, eggs and vanilla extract in a mixing bowl and whisk until the mixture is very light and has doubled in size. Whilst still whisking, slowly pour in the cooled chocolate and butter mixture.

Fold in the hazelnut flour and pour the mixture into the prepared tin/pan. Bake in the preheated oven for about 30–40 minutes, until the topping has formed a crust and a knife inserted in the middle of the brownie comes out clean. Let cool before cutting into squares to serve.

These brownies will keep for up to 5 days if stored in an airtight container.

For the flapjack base
125 g/1 stick plus 1 tablespoon butter
100 g/½ cup caster/granulated sugar
100 g/1 scant cup desiccated coconut
100 g/1 cup shelled pecans, finely chopped

For the brownie topping
125 g/1 stick plus 1 tablespoon butter
200 g/7 oz dark chocolate (70% cocoa solids)
125 g/⅔ cup caster/granulated sugar
125 g/½ cup plus 1 tablespoon dark soft brown sugar
3 eggs
1 teaspoon vanilla extract
100 g/1 cup hazelnut flour

a 33 x 23-cm/13 x 9-inch baking tin/pan, greased and base-lined

Makes 20 brownies

The cherry bakewell has been popular in England for many years. Buttery pastry is spread thickly with cherry jam and topped with a baked almond filling. Whilst traditionally made with ground almonds, this recipe is made with coconut, which gives a lovely texture and flavour. Look out for Baker's Angel Flake coconut, it's my preferred brand.

coconut bakewell slices

For the base

125 g/1 stick plus 1 tablespoon butter, softened

100 g/½ cup caster/granulated sugar

1 generous tablespoon golden/light corn syrup

150 g/2 cups long soft shredded coconut

50 g/⅓ cup coconut flour

250 g/1 cup cherry preserve

For the topping

100 g/7 tablespoons butter

100 g/½ cup caster/granulated sugar

3 eggs

50 g/⅓ cup gluten-free plain/all-purpose baking flour

50 g/⅓ cup coconut flour

100 g/1 cup ground almonds

150 g/2 cups desiccated coconut

2 tablespoons sour cream

a 30 x 20-cm/12 x 8-inch baking tin/pan, greased and base-lined

Makes 10 slices

Preheat the oven to 180°C (350°F) Gas 4.

To make the base, put the butter, sugar and syrup in a large saucepan and set over low heat until melted. Add the shredded coconut and coconut flour and mix well. Transfer the mixture to the prepared tin/pan and use the back of a spoon to press it down to cover the base of the tin/pan. Use a round-bladed knife to spread over the cherry preserve.

To make the coconut topping, put the butter and sugar in a mixing bowl and whisk until light and creamy. Beat in the eggs, then add both the flours, ground almonds, 100 g/generous 1 cup of the shredded coconut and sour cream and mix well.

Spoon the coconut topping over the preserve layer and spread out evenly. Sprinkle the remaining shredded coconut over the top. Bake in the preheated oven for 30–40 minutes, until golden brown and the topping is set. Remove from the oven and let cool in the tin/pan before cutting into slices to serve.

These slices are best eaten on the day they are made.

Gingerbread was my grandad's favourite cake and my mum would always bake a batch to take with us when we went to visit. I remember it being dark, sticky and laden with treacle/molasses and syrup – just how gingerbread should be.

apple & orange gingerbread

Preheat the oven to 180°C (350°F) Gas 4.

Put the butter, treacle/molasses, syrup and sugar in a saucepan and heat gently until the butter has melted and the sugar dissolved. Whisk in the milk, set aside to cool for 10 minutes then beat in the eggs.

Sift the flour into a mixing bowl and stir in the ground almonds, spices, bicarbonate of soda/baking soda, vanilla extract, orange zest, apple and almonds.

Pour the treacle mixture into the dry ingredients and mix well. Pour the batter into the prepared tin/pan and bake in the preheated oven for 30–40 minutes, until the gingerbread is firm to touch but still soft. Remove from the oven and let cool in the tin/pan. Dust with icing/confectioners' sugar and cut into squares to serve.

This gingerbread will keep for up to 3 days if stored in an airtight container.

115 g/1 stick butter
170 g/½ cup black treacle/ molasses
60 g/scant ¼ cup golden/light corn syrup
30 g/2 tablespoons dark soft brown sugar
125 ml/½ cup milk
2 eggs
115 g/¾ cup plus 1 tablespoon gluten-free plain/all-purpose baking flour
115 g/1 cup ground almonds
1 teaspoon mixed spice/apple pie spice
1 teaspoon ground cinnamon
2 teaspoons ground ginger
1 teaspoon bicarbonate of soda/ baking soda
1 teaspoon vanilla extract
finely grated zest of 2 small oranges
1 large apple, cored and grated
50 g/⅓ cup flaked/sliced almonds
icing/confectioners' sugar, for dusting

a 35 x 25-cm/14 x 10-inch cake tin/pan, greased and base-lined

Makes 16 squares

cakes

Everyone loves a cupcake. These are bursting with cranberries and white chocolate and topped with a pretty swirled buttermilk frosting – perfect for any celebration.

cranberry & white chocolate cupcakes

Preheat the oven to 180°C (350°F) Gas 4.

Put the butter and sugar in a mixing bowl and whisk until light and creamy. Add the egg and whisk again. Fold in the flour, baking powder, ground pecans, cranberries, chocolate buttons and buttermilk using a spatula or large spoon. Divide the batter between the paper cases. Bake in the preheated oven for 15–20 minutes, until the cakes are golden brown and spring back to the touch. Transfer to a wire rack to cool.

To make the frosting, sift the icing/confectioners' sugar into a mixing bowl and add the butter, vanilla extract and buttermilk. Beat together until you have a thick frosting. Put half the frosting in a separate bowl and mix in a few drops of pink food colouring. Spoon the frosting into the piping bag, spreading the pink one along one side of the bag and the cream one along the other side so that when you squeeze it the frosting is striped. Pipe a generous swirl of frosting onto each cooled cake, add some sprinkles and dust with icing/confectioners' sugar.

These cupcakes are best eaten on the day they are made.

60 g/½ stick butter, softened
60 g/⅓ cup caster/granulated sugar
1 egg
60 g gluten-free self-raising flour plus 1 teaspoon baking powder OR ½ cup gluten-free all-purpose baking flour plus 1½ teaspoons baking powder and ⅛ teaspoon xanthan gum
30 g/⅓ cup pecans, finely ground
60 g/½ cup dried cranberries
50 g/⅓ cup white chocolate buttons/chips
2 tablespoons buttermilk

For the frosting
220 g/1½ cups icing/confectioners' sugar
115 g/1 stick butter, softened
1 teaspoon vanilla extract
1 tablespoon buttermilk
pink food colouring
sprinkles of your choice

a 12-hole cupcake tin/pan, lined with 8 paper cases
a piping bag, fitted with a large star nozzle/tip

Makes 8

Red velvet cake – the signature dish of the Waldorf Astoria in New York in the 1920s – is coloured red to give it its distinctive look. Not quite a vanilla cake, not quite a chocolate cake, but most definitely delicious and a firm favourite with many people. Topped with a swirl of cream cheese frosting, these cupcakes are just impossible to resist!

red velvet cupcakes

115 g/1 stick butter

115 g/½ cup plus 1 tablespoon caster/granulated sugar

2 eggs

85 g gluten-free self-raising flour plus 1 teaspoon baking powder OR ¾ cup gluten-free all-purpose baking flour plus 2 teaspoons baking powder and ⅛ teaspoon xanthan gum

60 g/½ cup ground almonds

50 g/2 oz. dark chocolate, melted

150 ml/⅔ cup buttermilk

red food colouring

For the frosting

240 g/1¾ cups icing/confectioners' sugar

60 g/½ stick butter, softened

70 g/⅓ cup cream cheese

1 tablespoon buttermilk

gluten-free cocoa powder, for dusting

a 12-hole cupcake tin/pan, lined with paper cases

a piping bag fitted with a large star nozzle/tip

Makes 12 cupcakes

Preheat the oven to 180°C (350°F) Gas 4.

Put the butter and sugar in a mixing bowl and whisk until light and creamy. Add the eggs and whisk again. Fold in the flour, baking powder, ground almonds, melted chocolate and buttermilk using a spatula or large spoon. Beat in some red food colouring, a drop at a time, until the batter is a dark, reddish brown. Divide the cake batter between the paper cases. Bake in the preheated oven for 15–20 minutes, until the cakes are firm to the touch and a knife inserted into the middle of a cake comes out clean.

Transfer to a wire rack to cool.

To make the frosting, sift the icing/confectioners' sugar into a mixing bowl and add the butter, cream cheese and buttermilk. Beat together until you have a thick frosting. Spoon the frosting into the piping bag and pipe a large swirl on top of each cooled cake. Dust with a little sifted cocoa powder to decorate.

These cupcakes are best eaten on the day they are made.

There are few more pleasing cakes than the madeleine. Whilst they may look quite humble, flavour- and texture-wise they are a delight and ideal to serve with coffee or as an accompaniment to mousses and other creamy desserts. These are flavoured with honey, orange and cinnamon and eating them always transports me to the souks of Marrakesh. The secret to achieving the perfect texture is to chill the batter before baking – this helps the cakes to rise and be as light as a feather.

honey madeleines

Put the eggs and sugar in a mixing bowl and whisk until light and creamy. Sift in the flour and baking powder and add the hazelnuts, honey, orange zest and cinnamon. Whisk again. Pour in the cooled melted butter and fold in using a spatula until everything is incorporated. Spoon into a piping bag.

Chill the mixture in the fridge for 1 hour, taking care that the piping bag is well secured so that the mixture doesn't leak. The best way to do this is to wrap the open end of the nozzle in clingfilm/plastic wrap and then sit the piping bag upright in a large jug/pitcher.

Preheat the oven to 180°C (350°F) Gas 4. Pipe some of the mixture into each of the madeleine moulds/molds so that they are filled level. Bake in the preheated oven for 10–15 minutes, until golden brown. (If you have only one madeleine pan, bake in batches, storing the uncooked batter in the fridge whilst the first batch is cooking.) Gently remove the madeleines from the pan and transfer to a wire rack to cool. Dust with a little icing/confectioners' sugar whilst still warm.

These cakes are best eaten on the day they are made.

2 eggs

80 g/⅓ cup plus 2 tablespoons caster/granulated sugar

70 g gluten-free self-raising flour plus 1 teaspoon baking powder OR ½ cup plus 1 tablespoon gluten-free all-purpose baking flour plus 1½ teaspoons baking powder and ⅛ teaspoon xanthan gum

50 g/½ cup ground blanched hazelnuts

1 tablespoon honey

grated zest of 1 orange

1 teaspoon cinnamon

100 g/7 tablespoons butter, melted and cooled

icing/confectioners' sugar, for dusting

a piping bag, fitted with a large round nozzle/tip

2 madeleine tins/pans, very well greased with butter

Makes about 16

Lemon and almond are a match made in heaven. The drizzle ensures that these little loaf cakes stay nice and moist and the icing and almond topping finish them off to perfection.

lemon & amaretto loaf cakes

115 g/1 stick butter, softened

115g/½ cup plus 1 tablespoon caster/granulated sugar

2 large eggs

60 g gluten-free self-raising flour OR ½ cup gluten-free all-purpose baking flour plus ½ teaspoon baking powder and ⅛ teaspoon xanthan gum

60 g/½ cup ground almonds

80 ml/⅓ cup plain yogurt

grated zest of 2 lemons

For the drizzle

60 ml/¼ cup amaretto

1 tablespoon caster/superfine sugar

freshly squeezed juice of 2 lemons

For the icing

160 g/1 cup icing/confectioners' sugar

freshly squeezed juice of 2 lemons

flaked/sliced almonds, toasted

6 mini loaf tins/pans, greased and lined

Makes 6 mini loaf cakes

Preheat the oven to 180°C (350°F) Gas 4.

Put the butter and sugar in a mixing bowl and whisk until light and creamy. Add the eggs and whisk again. Fold in the flour, ground almonds, yogurt and lemon zest using a spatula. Put a large spoonful of cake batter into each prepared tin/pan. Bake in the preheated oven for about 20–25 minutes, until the cakes are firm to the touch and golden brown.

To make the drizzle, put the amaretto, sugar and lemon juice in a small saucepan and heat until the sugar has dissolved. Pour over the warm cakes and leave to cool in the tins/pans.

To make the icing, mix the icing/confectioner's sugar and lemon juice together, adding a little extra water if the icing is too stiff. Remove the cakes from the tins, spoon a little icing over the top of each cake and sprinkle with toasted almonds.

These cakes will keep for up to 2 days if stored in an airtight container.

My German friend Maren introduced me to the delights of buckwheat cake, delicate layers of almost marshmallow-like sponge filled with whipped cream and sour/tart cherries. This is a northern German twist on the classic and ever-popular Black Forest Gâteau.

buckwheat & cherry cake

Preheat the oven to 180°C (350°F) Gas 4.

Whisk together the egg yolks and sugar until thick, pale and creamy. In a separate grease-free bowl, whisk the egg whites to stiff peaks. Gently fold the egg whites into the egg yolk mixture. Mix together the flour and baking powder, sift over the egg mixture and gently fold in.

Pour the batter into the prepared baking tin/pan. Bake in the preheated oven for 30–40 minutes, until the cake is firm to the touch. It will feel foam-like rather than cake-like – almost like a giant marshmallow.

Carefully turn the cake out from the tin/pan onto a wire rack and let cool completely. Using a large, sharp knife, slice the cake into three layers. Drizzle each layer with kirsch, if using. Assemble the cake, filling each layer with whipped cream and cherries. Top the final layer with grated chocolate and serve immediately or cover and refrigerate until needed.

This cake is best eaten on the day it is made as it contains fresh cream. Refrigerate until ready to serve.

6 large eggs, separated

200 g/1 cup caster/superfine sugar

100 g/¾ cup buckwheat flour

2 teaspoons baking powder

kirsch, for drizzling (optional)

600 ml/2½ cups double/heavy cream, whipped to soft peaks

300 g/1 cup bottled or canned sour/tart morello cherries (drained weight)

3 tablespoons grated dark chocolate

a 23-cm/9-inch springform cake tin/pan, greased and lined

Serves 8–10

This moist carrot and coconut cake is so delicious that you wouldn't know it was gluten-free. The caramel, coconut and ginger topping is rich and buttery, making the cake perfect for dessert, served with a large spoonful of cream. The cake can be served warm or cold (although we tend to eat it as soon as it is removed from the oven as it always smells too delicious to resist).

carrot & coconut cake

170 g/1½ sticks butter, plus
    1 extra tablespoon for the
    topping
170 g/¾ cup plus 1 tablespoon
    caster/granulated sugar
3 eggs
170 g gluten-free self-raising flour
    OR 1⅓ cups gluten-free
    all-purpose baking flour plus
    1¼ teaspoons baking powder
    and ¾ teaspoon xanthan gum
200 g/2 scant cups long shredded
    coconut
2 carrots, grated
1 apple, cored and grated
85 g/½ cup sultanas/golden
    raisins
1 teaspoon ground cinnamon
1 teaspoon ground mixed spice/
    apple pie spice
200 ml/¾ cup buttermilk
1 tablespoon ginger syrup
2 tablespoons golden/light corn
    syrup

*a 20-cm/8-inch round springform
cake tin/pan, greased and lined*

Serves 8–10

Preheat the oven to 180°C (350°F) Gas 4.

Cream together the butter and sugar until light and creamy using an electric mixer or whisk. Add the eggs one at a time, beating after each addition. Fold in the flour, half of the shredded coconut, grated carrots and apple, sultanas/golden raisins, cinnamon, mixed spice/apple pie spice and buttermilk, ensuring that everything is incorporated.

Spoon the batter into the prepared tin/pan. Bake in the preheated oven for 40–55 minutes, until the cake is golden brown and springs back to the touch and a knife inserted in the middle comes out clean with no batter on it. If the cake starts to brown too quickly, cover loosely with a sheet of foil.

Meanwhile, to make the topping, put the tablespoonful of butter and both the syrups in a medium saucepan and heat gently until the butter has completely melted. Stir in the remaining shredded coconut and simmer for 2–3 minutes, until the coconut has absorbed some of the syrup.

Remove the cake from the oven, let it cool in the tin for 10 minutes and then turn out onto a wire rack to cool. Spoon the coconut topping evenly over the warm cake and let cool.

This cake will keep for up to 3 days if stored in an airtight container.

Here is a deliciously rich chocolate cake made with ground hazelnuts, which give the cake its nutty crunch. Lovers of Nutella hazelnut and chocolate spread will definitely enjoy a slice of this! Serve with freshly whipped cream for an extra-special treat!

chocolate hazelnut ring

Preheat the oven to 180°C (350°F) Gas 4.

Cream together the butter and sugar. Whisk in the eggs one at a time. Blitz the hazelnuts to a fine powder in a food processor or chop very finely with a sharp knife.

Add the ground hazelnuts, ground almonds, flour, baking powder, melted chocolate, vanilla extract and sour cream to the bowl and fold through with a spatula until everything is incorporated. Spoon into the prepared tin/pan and bake in the preheated oven for 30–40 minutes, until a knife inserted in the cake comes out clean.

Let the cake cool in the tin for 10 minutes then remove the sides and centre of the tin and let the cake cool on a wire rack. Drizzle the cake with the melted chocolate and sprinkle over the hazelnuts to decorate.

This cake is best eaten on the day it is made.

100 g/7 tablespoons butter, softened

140 g/scant ¾ cup caster/ granulated sugar

3 eggs

150 g/1½ cups blanched hazelnuts

100 g/1 cup ground almonds

60 g gluten-free self-raising flour plus 1 teaspoon baking powder OR ½ cup gluten-free all-purpose baking flour plus 1½ teaspoons baking powder and ⅛ teaspoon xanthan gum

140 g/5 oz dark chocolate, melted

1 teaspoon vanilla extract

3 tablespoons sour cream

To decorate

100 g/3½ oz dark chocolate, melted

50 g/½ cup blanched hazelnuts, toasted

a 23-cm/9-inch springform ring tin/pan, greased

Serves 10

I made this cake to take to our village harvest supper – a delightful event where we all enjoy a simple casserole followed by apple cakes and pies for dessert, and an auction of homegrown produce for charity. The cake is topped with my friend Susan's caramel icing – so delicious that I just begged for the recipe until she gave in!

apple & pecan cake

200 g/2 cups shelled pecans

225 g/2 sticks butter, softened

115 g/½ cup caster/granulated
   sugar

115 g/½ cup dark soft brown
   sugar

4 eggs

150 g gluten-free self-raising flour
   plus 1 teaspoon baking powder
   OR 1 cup and 2 tablespoons
   gluten-free all-purpose baking
   flour plus 2 teaspoons baking
   powder and ¼ teaspoon
   xanthan gum

2 teaspoons ground cinnamon

2 apples

100 ml/⅓ cup sour cream

For the icing

60 g/½ stick butter

150 g/¾ cup caster/superfine
   sugar

2 tablespoons milk

2 teaspoons vanilla extract

220 g/1½ cups icing/
   confectioners' sugar

ground cinnamon, for dusting

*a 25-cm/10-inch springform tin/
pan, greased and lined*

Serves 10

Preheat the oven to 170°C (325°F) Gas 3.

Blitz the pecans in a food processor until they resemble ground almonds. Whisk together the butter and both sugars until light and creamy. Add the eggs and whisk again. Fold in the flour, baking powder, cinnamon and ground pecans using a spatula or spoon.

Peel, grate and core the apples and fold through the batter, along with the sour cream. Spoon the batter into the prepared cake tin/pan and bake in the preheated oven for 1–1¼ hours, until the cake is firm to the touch and a knife inserted into the middle of the cake comes out clean. Let cool in the tin/pan for a few minutes then turn out onto a wire rack and let cool.

To make the icing, put the butter and sugar in a saucepan and heat gently until the butter has melted and the sugar starts to caramelize. Add the milk and vanilla extract and heat for 1 minute further. Remove from the heat, let cool for 5 minutes, then beat in the icing/confectioners' sugar using a whisk. Spread the icing over the cooled cake using a spatula and sift over a little ground cinnamon.

This cake will keep for up to 5 days if stored in an airtight container.

Tangy lemon slices, drenched in a lemon caramel, nestled on top of
a delicate lemon sponge, make this cake a must for all citrus lovers.
Delicious served warm with custard sauce or cold with whipped cream.

caramelized lemon cake

Preheat the oven to 180°C (350°F) Gas 4.

To make the caramelized lemons, put the sugar and lemon juice in a saucepan
and heat until the sugar melts and turns golden brown. Do not stir whilst cooking but
gently shake the pan from time to time to prevent the sugar from burning. Watch
closely once the sugar has melted as it will caramelize quickly. Pour into the bottom
of the pan. Grate the zest from 3 of the lemons and reserve for the cake batter. Cut
the top and bottom from all 5 lemons and stand them upright on a chopping board.
Using a sharp knife slice away the peel and pith in vertical slices and repeat until the
lemons are peeled. Cut each lemon into 6 slices and remove any pips using a sharp
knife. Arrange the lemon slices in the caramel in the pan in a circular pattern – taking
care as the caramel will be hot. Set aside.

Put the butter and sugar in a mixing bowl and whisk together until light and
creamy. Beat in the eggs and whisk again until the batter is light and airy. Sift in the
flour and baking powder and add the ground almonds, sour cream and reserved
lemon zest. Fold together until everything is incorporated. Spoon the batter into the
pan with the lemon slices. Bake in the preheated oven for 30–40 minutes, until the
cake springs back to the touch and a knife inserted in the middle of the cake comes
out clean. Remove from the oven and let cool for a few minutes then put a serving
plate on top of the pan and, holding the pan with a kitchen towel (so you do not burn
yourself) invert the cake onto the plate. Serve warm or cold with custard sauce or
whipped cream.

This cake will keep for up to 2 days if stored in an airtight container.

170 g/1½ sticks butter, softened

170 g/¾ cup plus 2 tablespoons
caster/granulated sugar

3 large eggs

115 g gluten-free self-raising flour
plus 1 teaspoon baking powder
OR heaped ¾ cup gluten-free
all-purpose baking flour plus
2 teaspoons baking powder
and ¼ teaspoon xanthan gum

85 g/¾ cup ground almonds

3 tablespoons sour cream

custard sauce or whipped cream,
to serve

For the caramelized lemons

200 g/1 cup caster/granulated
sugar

freshly squeezed juice of 1 lemon

4 lemons

*a 25-cm/10-inch cast iron tarte
tatin pan or a similar heavy,
flameproof tin/pan, greased*

Serves 8–10

The classic victoria sponge remains the most popular of traditional teatime treats. Light vanilla sponge cakes are sandwiched together with buttercream and strawberry preserve. My recipe replaces the buttercream with fluffy whipped cream and fresh, juicy strawberries for an indulgent treat.

victoria sponge cake

185 g/1 stick plus 5 tablespoons butter, softened

185 g/1 cup less 1 tablespoon caster/granulated sugar

4 eggs

200 g/2 cups ground almonds

125 g gluten-free self-raising flour OR 1 scant cup gluten-free all-purpose baking flour plus 1 teaspoon baking powder and ¼ teaspoon xanthan gum

150 ml/⅔ cup sour cream

2 teaspoons vanilla extract

To assemble

3 generous tablespoons strawberry preserve

250 ml/1 cup double/heavy cream, whipped

150 g/2 cups hulled and sliced strawberries

icing/confectioners' sugar, for dusting

2 x 20-cm/8-inch cake tins/pans, greased and lined

Serves 10

Preheat the oven to 180°C (350°F) Gas 4.

Put the butter and sugar in a mixing bowl and whisk until light and creamy. Add the eggs one at a time, whisking after each addition. Add the ground almonds, flour, sour cream and vanilla extract and fold through gently. Spoon the mixture into the prepared cake tins/pans and level using a spatula.

Bake in the preheated oven for 25–30 minutes, until the cakes are firm to the touch and a knife inserted into the middle of each cake comes out clean. Turn out onto a wire rack and let cool completely.

Spread the preserve over one of the cakes. Cover with the whipped cream and strawberry slices and top with the other sponge. Dust with icing/confectioners' sugar and serve immediately or refrigerate until needed.

This cake is best eaten on the day it is made as it contains fresh cream. Refrigerate until ready to serve.

Ripe juicy plums, bursting blueberries and warming cinnamon – this good-looking cake is delicious served with chilled pouring cream.

plum & cinnamon cake

Preheat the oven to 160°C (325°F) Gas 3.

Put the butter and sugar in a mixing bowl and whisk until light and creamy. Add the eggs one at a time, whisking after each addition. Sift in the flour and cinnamon, add the ground almonds and whisk again. Spoon the batter into the prepared cake tin/pan and level the surface.

Arrange the plums, cut-side up, over the top of the cake, scatter over the blueberries and sprinkle with the sugar.

Bake in the preheated oven for 1½–2 hours, until the cake is firm to the touch and a knife inserted into the middle of the cake comes out clean.

Remove from the oven and let cool in the tin/pan for 10 minutes, then turn out onto a wire rack to cool completely. Dust with icing/confectioner's sugar and serve with whipped cream.

This cake will keep for up to 3 days if stored in an airtight container.

185 g/1½ sticks plus 1 tablespoon butter, softened
275 g/1½ cups caster/granulated sugar
6 eggs
125 g gluten-free self-raising flour OR 1 scant cup gluten-free all-purpose baking flour plus 1 teaspoon baking powder and ¼ teaspoon xanthan gum
2 teaspoons ground cinnamon
400 g/4½ cups ground almonds
pouring cream, to serve

For the topping
8 ripe plums, halved and pitted
100 g/1 cup blueberries
2 tablespoons caster/granulated sugar
icing/confectioners' sugar, for dusting

a 25-cm/10-inch springform tin/ pan, greased and lined

Serves 10

Banana bread is always popular, especially when served warm from the oven in thick slices and generously spread with butter. The addition of brazil nuts here gives this loaf cake a lovely texture but you can substitute any nuts you prefer – pistachios or hazelnuts both work well.

banana & brazil nut loaf cake

2 ripe bananas

115 g/1 stick butter, softened

115 g/½ cup plus 1 tablespoon caster/granulated sugar

2 large eggs

115 g gluten-free self-raising flour OR 1 scant cup gluten-free all-purpose baking flour plus 1 teaspoon baking powder and ¼ teaspoon xanthan gum

3 tablespoons buttermilk

2 teaspoons ground cinnamon

1 teaspoon ground mixed spice/apple pie spice

100 g/1 cup brazil nuts, coarsely chopped

For the caramel glaze

1 tablespoon butter

1 tablespoon light soft brown sugar

1 tablespoon golden/light corn syrup

¼ teaspoon fine sea salt

2 x 450-g/1-lb loaf tins/pans, greased and lined

Makes 2 loaf cakes

Preheat the oven to 180°C (350°F) Gas 4.

Put the bananas in a bowl and mash with a fork. Put the butter and sugar in a mixing bowl and whisk until light and creamy. Add the eggs one at a time, whisking after each addition. Add the mashed banana, flour, buttermilk, cinnamon, mixed spice/apple pie spice and brazil nuts and fold in until everything is incorporated.

Divide the batter between the prepared loaf tins/pans and bake in the preheated oven for 25–30 minutes, until the cakes are firm to the touch and a knife inserted in the middle of each cake comes out clean. Remove the loaves from the oven and let cool slightly while you make the glaze.

To make the salted caramel glaze, heat the butter, sugar, syrup and salt in a saucepan until the butter has melted and the sugar dissolved. Drizzle the caramel over the warm cakes to glaze and leave for a few minutes before turning out onto a wire rack to cool.

These cakes will keep for up to 3 days if stored in an airtight container. They also freeze very well, so if you don't need both cakes, you can freeze one for up to 2 months.

This light almond sponge cake, topped with fresh peaches and crunchy nuts, makes a comforting dessert served with whipped cream or custard sauce. I use Spanish Marcona almonds as their rich smoky taste really enhances the sweetness of the peaches.

peach & almond cake

Preheat the oven to 180°C (350°F) Gas 4.

Put the butter and 170 g/¾ cup of the sugar in a mixing bowl and cream together. Whisk in the eggs one at a time. Add the flour, ground almonds and buttermilk and fold together with a large spoon. Add the orange juice, zest and vanilla extract and mix until everything is incorporated.

Spoon the cake batter into the prepared tin/pan and arrange the peach slices evenly over the top of the cake. Sprinkle over the almonds and remaining sugar and bake in the preheated oven for 30–40 minutes, until a knife inserted into the middle comes out clean.

Put the lemon juice and peach preserve in a small saucepan and heat gently until the preserve has melted. Strain through a fine mesh sieve/ strainer and use a pastry brush to brush it over the top of the cake to glaze. Let the cake cool in the tin/pan then cut into slices to serve.

This cake will keep for up to 2 days if stored in an airtight container.

170 g/1 stick plus 4 tablespoons butter, softened

200 g/1 cup caster/granulated sugar

3 large eggs

115 g gluten-free self-raising flour OR ¾ cup plus 1 tablespoon gluten-free all-purpose baking powder plus 1 teaspoon baking powder and ½ teaspoon xanthan gum

145 g/1½ cups ground almonds

150 ml/⅔ cup buttermilk

freshly squeezed juice and zest of 1 small orange

1 teaspoon vanilla extract

4 ripe peaches, pitted and sliced

60 g/⅓ cup large whole blanched almonds, such as Marcona

For the glaze

freshly squeezed juice of 2 lemons

3 tablespoons peach preserve

a 30 x 20-cm/12 x 8-inch rectangular flan tin/pan, greased and lined

Serves 8–10

The flavours of almond and chocolate complement each other perfectly in this delicious cake. Sandwiched together with a rich buttercream, this bake would be the ideal centrepiece for afternoon tea or perfect to serve with morning coffee.

almond & chocolate chip layer cake

225 g/2 sticks butter, softened

225 g/1 cup plus 2 tablespoons caster/granulated sugar

4 eggs, lightly beaten

150 g gluten-free self-raising flour plus 2 teaspoons baking powder OR 1 cup and 2 tablespoons gluten-free all-purpose baking flour plus 3 teaspoons baking powder and ¼ teaspoon xanthan gum

115 g/1 generous cup ground almonds

2 teaspoons almond extract

100 g/⅔ cup chocolate chips

100 ml/⅓ cup buttermilk

For the buttercream

60 g/2½ oz. dark chocolate

115 g/1 stick butter, softened

220 g/1½ cups icing/confectioners' sugar, plus extra for dusting

1 tablespoon buttermilk

2 x 20-cm/8-inch round cake tins/pans, greased and lined

a piping bag, fitted with a large round nozzle (optional)

Serves 8–10

Preheat the oven to 180°C (350°F) Gas 4.

Put the butter and sugar in a mixing bowl and whisk together until light and creamy. Add the eggs and whisk again. Sift in the flour and baking powder and add the ground almonds. Use a spatula to fold in. Add the almond extract, chocolate chips and buttermilk and mix until everything is incorporated.

Divide the cake batter between the prepared cake tins/pans. Bake in the preheated oven for 25–35 minutes, until the cakes are golden brown, firm to the touch and a knife inserted in the middle of each cake comes out clean. Transfer to a wire rack to cool.

To make the filling, break the chocolate into pieces and put in a heatproof bowl set over a saucepan of barely simmering water. Take care that the base of the bowl does not touch the water. Stir until the chocolate has melted. Take the bowl off the heat and let the chocolate cool. Whisk in the butter, icing/confectioners' sugar and buttermilk until smooth. Spoon the buttercream into the piping bag and pipe stars on one cake. (If you do not have a piping bag, spread the filling over the cake with a round-bladed knife.) Top with the second cake and lighty dust with icing/confectioners' sugar to serve.

This cake will keep for up to 2 days if stored in an airtight container.

muffins
& scones

These little muffins are bursting with fresh blueberries and zingy lemon and have a hidden layer of cream cheese to make them nice and moist. Perfect for brunch or afternoon tea.

blueberry & lemon muffins

Preheat the oven to 180°C (350°F) Gas 4.

Put the butter and sugar in a mixing bowl and whisk together until light and creamy. Add the eggs and whisk again. Fold in the flour, baking powder, bicarbonate of soda/baking soda, ground almonds, buttermilk, lemon zest and blueberries. Put a spoonful of batter in each paper case to half fill it and then put 1 teaspoon of cream cheese in each one. Top with another spoonful of the cake batter, ensuring that the cream cheese is completely covered.

Bake in the preheated oven for about 15–20 minutes, until the muffins are firm to the touch.

To make the lemon drizzle, heat the lemon juice in a small saucepan with the icing/confectioners' sugar and pour over the muffins whilst they are still warm. Let the muffins cool in the tin/pan before serving.

These muffins are best eaten on the day they are made.

115 g/1 stick butter, softened
115 g/½ cup plus 2 tablespoons caster/granulated sugar
2 eggs, beaten
85 g gluten-free self-raising flour plus 1 teaspoon baking powder OR ¾ cup gluten-free all-purpose baking flour plus 2 teaspoons baking powder and ¼ teaspoon xanthan gum
1 teaspoon bicarbonate of soda/baking soda
60 g/¾ cup ground almonds
80 ml/⅓ cup buttermilk
grated zest of 2 lemons
100 g/1 cup blueberries
3 tablespoons cream cheese
freshly squeezed juice of 2 lemons
3 tablespoons icing/confectioners' sugar

a 12-hole muffin tin/pan, lined with 12 paper cases

Makes 12

Cornmeal flour gives these delicious muffins a lovely golden colour. Bursting with fresh apricots, chocolate and cherries and brushed with an apricot butter glaze, they are great for lunchboxes and picnics.

apricot cornmeal muffins

100 g/¾ cup cornmeal flour

150 g gluten-free self-raising flour plus 1 teaspoon baking powder OR 1⅓ cups gluten-free all-purpose baking flour plus 2¼ teaspoons baking powder and ¾ teaspoon xanthan gum

100 g/½ cup caster/granulated sugar

100 g/1 cup ground almonds

200 ml/¾ cup milk

1 teaspoon vanilla extract

2 generous tablespoons plain Greek yogurt

100 g/7 tablespoons butter, melted and cooled

2 large eggs

2 tablespoons apricot preserve

7 fresh apricots

75 g/½ cup dried sour cherries

100 g/3½ oz dark chocolate, finely chopped

For the apricot glaze

2 tablespoons apricot preserve

1 tablespoon butter

a 12-hole muffin tin/pan, lined with paper cases

Makes 12

Preheat the oven to 180°C (350°F) Gas 4.

Put the cornmeal flour, flour, baking powder, sugar and ground almonds in a mixing bowl.

Put the milk, vanilla extract, yogurt and melted butter in a separate bowl and whisk together. Add the eggs and apricot preserve to the milk mixture and whisk again. Pour the milk mixture into the bowl containing the dry ingredients and fold in with a large spoon.

Pit the apricots and chop 5 of them into small pieces. Stir the chopped apricots, cherries and chocolate into the batter. Divide the batter between the paper cases. Cut the remaining apricots into thin slices and arrange 2 on top of each muffin. Bake in the preheated oven for 15–20 minutes, until risen and golden brown.

To make the glaze, heat the apricot preserve and butter in a small saucepan and then brush over the warm muffins with a pastry brush. Leave to cool slightly then transfer to a wire rack to cool completely.

These muffins are best eaten on the day they are made.

When autumn/fall comes, I take a basket and head to the hedgerows. There is nothing nicer than picking free produce such as blackberries, hips and crab apples. This delicious recipe uses ripe blackberries with seasonal pears for a rustic scone that's perfect served warm with plenty of creamy butter.

pear & blackberry scone round

Preheat the oven to 190°C (375°F) Gas 5.

Put the flour, baking powder, ground almonds, cinnamon and salt in a large mixing bowl and stir together.

Add the butter and rub into the flour with your fingertips, until the mixture resembles fine breadcrumbs. Add the sugar and buttermilk and mix to form a soft dough, adding a little milk if the mixture is too dry. Add the blackberries and pear slices and gently bring the dough together with your hands.

Put the dough on a floured work surface and shape it into a 23-cm/9-in diameter round. Transfer to the prepared baking sheet using a large spatula. Brush the scone round with the beaten egg and sprinkle with a little extra sugar. Using a sharp knife, score the top of the scone into 8 sections but do not cut all the way through the dough. Bake in the preheated oven for 20–25 minutes, until golden brown and the scone sounds hollow when you tap it. Serve warm with butter for spreading.

This scone round is best eaten on the day it is made.

225 g gluten-free self-raising flour plus 1 teaspoon baking powder OR 1¾ cups gluten-free all-purpose baking flour plus 2 teaspoons baking powder and ½ teaspoon xanthan gum

200 g/2 cups ground almonds

2 teaspoons ground cinnamon

½ teaspoon fine sea salt

115 g/1 stick butter, chilled and cubed

55 g/¼ cup caster/granulated sugar, plus extra for sprinkling

200 ml/¾ cup buttermilk

200 g/1 cup blackberries

2 ripe pears, peeled, cored and sliced

1 egg, beaten

a baking sheet, greased and lined

Makes 8 slices

I was first introduced to pumpkin scones at the wonderful Alice's Tea Rooms in New York and have been hooked ever since. The pumpkin purée, flavoured with maple syrup, cinnamon and vanilla, is what makes these scones really moist.

pumpkin scones

300 g/10 oz peeled pumpkin or butternut squash, chopped into 3-cm/1¼-in pieces

40 ml/3 tablespoons pure maple syrup

2 tablespoons vanilla extract

1 teaspoon ground cinnamon

350 g gluten-free self-raising flour plus 1 teaspoon baking powder OR 2½ cups plus 1 tablespoon gluten-free all-purpose baking flour plus 3 teaspoons baking powder and 1 teaspoon xanthan gum

100 g/1 cup ground almonds

115 g/1 stick butter

50 g/¼ cup caster/granulated sugar

For the maple glaze

40 ml/3 tablespoons maple syrup

20 g/1 tablespoon butter

40 g/scant ¼ cup caster/ granulated sugar

1 teaspoon vanilla extract

a baking sheet, greased and lined

a 7.5-cm/3-inch fluted cutter

Makes 14

Preheat the oven to 190°C (375°F) Gas 5.

Put the pumpkin pieces on a large piece of double layer of kitchen foil. Drizzle over the maple syrup and vanilla extract and sprinkle with the cinnamon. Wrap the foil up well and transfer to a baking sheet. Bake in the preheated oven for 30–40 minutes, until the pumpkin is soft. Let cool, then purée until smooth in a food processor.

Put the flour, baking powder and ground almonds in a mixing bowl and rub in the butter with your fingertips. Add half the pumpkin purée and sugar to the flour and mix in. Gradually add the remaining purée a little at a time, until you have a soft dough. You may not need all the purée, depending on the water content of your pumpkin.

Put the dough on a floured work surface and use a rolling pin to roll out the scone dough to a thickness of 2–3 cm/¾–1¼ inches. Stamp out 14 rounds using the cutter. Arrange the scones on the prepared baking sheet a small distance apart. Bake in the preheated oven for 12–15 minutes, until the scones are golden brown and sound hollow when you tap them.

To make the glaze, put the maple syrup, butter, sugar and vanilla extract in a small saucepan and gently heat until the butter has melted and the sugar dissolves. Brush the glaze over the warm scones using a pastry brush. Serve warm or cold.

These scones are best eaten on the day they are made but can be frozen and reheated before serving.

The classic English teatime scone is so simple to make but always very popular. Split and topped with cream and strawberry jam/jelly, these treats represent everything that is lovely about the British summertime.

buttermilk scones

Preheat the oven to 190°C (375°F) Gas 5.

Put the flour, baking powder and ground almonds in a mixing bowl and rub in the butter with your fingertips. Add the sugar and almond extract and mix in the buttermilk, until you have a soft dough (you may not need all of it so add it gradually).

Put the dough on a floured work surface and use a rolling pin to roll it out to a thickness of 2–3 cm/¾–1¼ inches. Stamp out 12 scones using the cutter. Arrange the scones on the prepared baking sheet so that they are a distance apart. Brush the tops with milk and sprinkle with a little caster/granulated sugar. Bake in the preheated oven for 15–20 minutes, until golden brown and the scones sound hollow when you tap them. Transfer to a wire rack to cool.

To serve, cut the scones in half, spoon some cream on the base of each one, top with preserve and strawberry slices and cover with the tops of the scones. Dust with icing/confectioners' sugar to serve.

These scones are best eaten on the day they are made but can be frozen and reheated before serving.

Variation Try adding 85 g/½ cup dried cherries, sultanas/golden raisins or chocolate chips to the scone dough (replacing the almond extract with vanilla extract).

350 g gluten-free self-raising flour plus 2 teaspoons baking powder OR 2½ cups plus 1 tablespoon gluten-free all-purpose baking flour plus 4 teaspoons baking powder and 1 teaspoon xanthan gum
100 g/1¼ cups ground almonds
115 g/1 stick butter
60 g/⅓ cup caster/granulated sugar, plus extra for sprinkling
2 teaspoons almond extract
200–250 ml/¾–1 cup buttermilk
milk, for glazing

To serve
300 g/1 cup clotted cream
3 generous tablespoons strawberry preserve
icing/confectioners' sugar, to dust

a baking sheet, greased and lined
a 7.5-cm/3-inch fluted cutter

Makes 12

These muffins are bursting with tomato and make a delicious savoury snack, or are delicious served on the side of a bowl of soup or a fresh salad. The added delights of feta and fresh basil will transport you to the Mediterranean and sunny days.

tomato, basil & feta muffins

350 g gluten-free self-raising flour plus 1 teaspoon baking powder OR 2¾ cups gluten-free all-purpose flour plus 4 teaspoons baking powder and 2 teaspoons xanthan gum

1 teaspoon bicarbonate of soda/ baking soda

250 ml/1 cup milk

250 ml/1 cup plain yogurt

2 eggs

100 g/6½ tablespoons butter, melted and cooled

2 tablespoons tomato purée/ paste

160 g/¾ cup (drained weight) sundried tomatoes preserved in oil, chopped, plus one tablespoon of the oil

200 g/7 oz. feta cheese, chopped into small pieces

3 tablespoons chopped fresh basil leaves

sea salt and ground black pepper

3 x 6-hole muffin pans lined with 16 paper cases

Makes 16

Preheat the oven to 180°C (350°F) Gas 4.

Sift the flour, baking powder (plus xanthan gum, if using) and bicarbonate of soda/ baking soda into a large mixing bowl.

In a separate bowl, whisk together the milk, yogurt, eggs, melted butter and tomato purée/paste, then add this to the flour mixture. Whisk everything together well and season with salt and pepper. Mix the tomatoes and feta cheese into the mixture, along with the tomato oil and the chopped basil.

Divide the mixture between the muffin cases, making sure that some of the pieces of cheese and sundried tomato sit on the top of each muffin. Bake the muffins in the preheated oven for 20–30 minutes until golden brown. Serve warm or cold.

The muffins will keep for up to 2 days in an airtight container, but can be frozen and then reheated to serve.

These lovely muffins are an ideal accompaniment to tomato soup. Packed with both puréed corn and whole kernels, they are deliciously moist and full of flavour.

sweetcorn muffins

Preheat the oven to 180°C (350°F) Gas 4.

Sift the flour, baking powder (plus xanthan gum, if using) and bicarbonate of soda/baking soda into a mixing bowl and stir in the cornmeal.

Blitz half of the sweetcorn/corn kernels to a smooth purée in a food processor, and add it to the flour mixture.

In a separate bowl, whisk together the milk, eggs, crème fraîche and melted butter, then add to the flour mixture. Whisk everything together well, adding the sugar and seasoning with salt and pepper. Stir through most of the remaining whole sweetcorn/corn kernels, reserving a few kernels to sprinkle on top of the muffins.

Divide the mixture between the muffin cases and top with the remaining corn. Bake in the preheated oven for 25–30 minutes until golden brown and the muffins spring back to your touch. Serve warm or cold.

The muffins will keep for up to 2 days in an airtight container but can be frozen and then reheated to serve.

200 g gluten-free self-raising flour plus 1 teaspoon baking powder OR 1⅔ cups gluten-free all-purpose flour plus 2¾ teaspoons baking powder and 1¼ teaspoons xanthan gum

1 teaspoon bicarbonate of soda/baking soda

50 g/⅓ cup fine cornmeal

330 g/1⅔ cups sweetcorn/corn kernels

150 ml/⅔ cup milk

2 eggs

4 tablespoons/¼ cup crème fraîche or sour cream

100 g/6½ tablespoons butter, melted and cooled

1 tablespoon caster/granulated sugar

sea salt and ground black pepper

3 x 6-hole muffin pans lined with 16 paper cases

Makes 16

These dense muffins are kept really soft and moist with the addition of mashed potato. Sage has quite a strong flavour and if you are not keen on it you can substitute 2 tablespoons of finely chopped chives instead, adding them to the potato with the melted butter.

sage & potato muffins

400 g/14 oz. potatoes, peeled and chopped

165 g/1 stick plus 3 tablespoons butter

15 small sage leaves, cut into thin strips

1 tablespoon caster/granulated sugar

2 eggs

115 g gluten-free self-raising flour plus 2 teaspoons baking powder OR scant 1 cup gluten-free all-purpose flour plus 3 teaspoons baking powder and ¾ teaspoon xanthan gum

2 tablespoons crème fraîche or sour cream

2 x 6-hole muffin pans lined with 12 paper cases

Makes 12

Boil the potatoes in salted water for about 20 minutes until soft.

Preheat the oven to 180°C (350°F) Gas 4.

Heat 50 g/3½ tablespoons of the butter in a frying pan and fry the sage leaves until crispy. Pour the melted sage butter over the cooked potatoes and mash with a potato masher until smooth, then leave to cool.

Whisk together the remaining butter and the sugar in a large mixing bowl. Add the eggs, flour, baking powder (plus xanthan gum, if using), crème fraîche and cooled potato and whisk until the batter is smooth. Spoon the mixture into the muffin cases and bake in the preheated oven for 35–45 minutes until the muffins are golden brown.

These muffins are best served warm on the day that they are baked.

If you are more of a savoury than sweet person, then these are the scones for you. Packed with cheese and walnuts and with the satisfying crunch of poppy seeds, they are delicious served as an accompaniment to a hearty bowl of broccoli soup.

cheese & poppy seed scones

Preheat the oven to 190°C (375°F) Gas 5.

Put the flour, baking powder and ground almonds in a mixing bowl and rub in the butter with your fingertips. Add the grated cheese, walnuts, poppy seeds and mustard and stir in. Mix in the buttermilk, until you have a soft dough (you may not need all of it so add it gradually).

Put the dough on a floured work surface and use a rolling pin to roll it out to a thickness of 2–3 cm/¾-1¼ inches. Stamp out 12 rounds using the cutter. Arrange the scones on the prepared baking sheet a small distance apart, brush the tops with the beaten egg and sprinkle with poppy seeds. Bake in the preheated oven for 15–20 minutes, until the scones are golden and sound hollow when you tap them. Serve warm or cold.

These scones are best eaten on the day they are made but can be frozen and reheated before serving.

350 g gluten-free self-raising flour plus 2 teaspoons baking powder OR 2½ cups plus 1 tablespoon gluten-free all-purpose baking flour plus 4 teaspoons baking powder and 1 teaspoon xanthan gum, plus extra flour for dusting

100 g/1 cup ground almonds

115 g/1 stick butter, chilled and cubed

200 g/1½ cups grated Cheddar

100 g/1 cup walnut halves, finely chopped

2 tablespoons poppy seeds, plus extra for sprinkling

1 generous teaspoon French mustard

200–250 ml/¾–1 cup buttermilk

1 egg yolk, beaten

a baking sheet, greased and lined

a 7.5-cm/3-inch round fluted scone/biscuit cutter

Makes 12 scones

savoury
pies & tarts

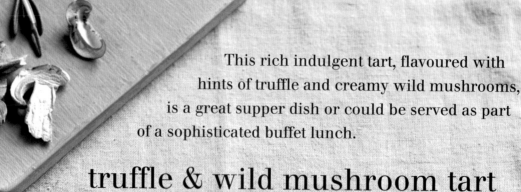

This rich indulgent tart, flavoured with
hints of truffle and creamy wild mushrooms,
is a great supper dish or could be served as part
of a sophisticated buffet lunch.

truffle & wild mushroom tart

Begin by preparing the filling as the mushrooms need to cool before being used in the tart. Drain the soaked porcini mushrooms and chop into small pieces, rinsing to remove any grit.

Melt the butter in a large frying pan and add the fresh mushrooms, rehydrated porcini, whole garlic cloves, rosemary and thyme. Cook over gentle heat for about 5 minutes until the mushrooms are soft and smell earthy. Season with truffle salt and pepper and leave to cool.

To make the pastry, rub the butter into the flour using your fingertips, then add the cream cheese, truffle oil and salt and bring together into a soft ball of dough, adding 1–2 tablespoons water if the mixture is too dry. Wrap the pastry dough in clingfilm/plastic wrap and chill in the refrigerator for 1 hour.

On a flour-dusted surface, roll out the pastry to a large rectangle just bigger than the size of the tart pan and use it to line the pan. Press the pastry in firmly with your fingers and trim away any excess using a sharp knife. If the pastry breaks, don't worry, just patch any holes with the pastry trimmings. Prick the base with the prongs of a fork and chill in the refrigerator for a further 30 minutes.

Preheat the oven to 180°C (350°F) Gas 4.

Line the pastry case with non-stick baking paper, fill with baking beans and bake for about 15–20 minutes until the pastry is golden brown. Remove the tart case from the oven and leave to cool slightly. Remove the baking paper and baking beans. Turn the oven temperature down to 120°C (250°F) Gas ½.

Whisk together the whole eggs, egg yolks and cream, season with the truffle salt and pepper, then pour the mixture into the pastry case. Remove the garlic cloves and rosemary and thyme sprigs from the mushroom mixture, then sprinkle the mushrooms over the filling – they will sink into the filling slightly but will still be visible on top. Carefully transfer the tart to the oven and bake for about 1½ hours until the top of the tart is lightly golden brown and the filling is just set with a slight wobble in the centre. Leave to cool and then chill in the refrigerator until you are ready to serve.

The tart will keep for up to 3 days in the refrigerator in an airtight container or covered in clingfilm/plastic wrap.

For the pastry

75 g/5 tablespoons butter, chilled and cubed

190 g/1½ cups gluten-free plain/all-purpose flour, sifted, plus extra for dusting

75 g/5 tablespoons cream cheese

1 tablespoon truffle oil

¼ teaspoon salt

For the mushroom filling

25 g/1 oz. dried porcini mushrooms, soaked in hot water

50 g/3½ tablespoons butter

375 g/13 oz. mushrooms (such as button and chestnut/cremini), roughly chopped

2 garlic cloves, peeled

1 sprig of fresh rosemary

3 sprigs of fresh thyme

2 whole eggs, plus 3 egg yolks

400 ml/1⅔ cups double/heavy cream

truffle salt (or if not available regular sea salt) and ground black pepper

a 25-cm/10-inch loose-based tart pan, greased

baking beans

Serves 8

When asparagus is in first season, this recipe is perfect to make the most of this delicious vegetable. With a lemon cream filling and cream cheese pastry, this tart makes an elegant supper dish.

asparagus tart

For the pastry
75 g/5 tablespoons butter, chilled
    and cubed
190 g/1½ cups gluten-free plain/
    all-purpose flour, sifted, plus
    extra for dusting
75 g/5 tablespoons cream cheese
¼ teaspoon salt

For the filling
250 g/9 oz. asparagus
5 egg yolks
300 ml/1¼ cups whipping cream
grated zest of 1 lemon
sea salt and ground black pepper

a 30 x 18-cm/12 x 7-inch
loose-based tart pan, greased
baking beans

Serves 8

Trim any woody ends from the asparagus spears, then blanch them in a pan of boiling, salted water for about 3 minutes until just soft. Plunge into iced water and leave until you are ready to fill the tart.

To make the pastry, rub the butter into the flour using your fingertips, then add the cream cheese and salt and bring together into a soft ball of dough, adding 1–2 tablespoons water if the mixture is too dry. Wrap the pastry dough in clingfilm/plastic wrap and chill in the refrigerator for 1 hour.

On a flour-dusted surface, roll out the pastry to 2–3 mm/⅛ inch thick and use it to line the tart pan. Press the pastry in firmly with your fingers and trim away any excess using a sharp knife. If the pastry breaks, don't worry, just patch any holes with the pastry trimmings. Prick the base and chill in the refrigerator for a further 30 minutes.

Preheat the oven to 180°C (350°F) Gas 4.

Line the pastry case with non-stick baking paper, fill with baking beans and bake for about 15–20 minutes until the pastry is golden brown. Remove the tart case from the oven and leave to cool slightly. Remove the baking paper and baking beans. Turn the oven temperature down to 120°C (250°F) Gas ½.

Whisk together the egg yolks, cream and lemon zest and season with salt and pepper, then slowly pour the mixture into the pastry case. Arrange the asparagus spears in a decorative pattern in the tart. They will sink into the filling slightly but will still be visible on top. Carefully transfer the tart to the oven and bake for about 1½ hours until the top of the tart is lightly golden brown and the filling is just set with a slight wobble in the centre. Leave to cool, then chill in the refrigerator until you are ready to serve.

The tart will keep for up to 3 days in the refrigerator in an airtight container or covered in clingfilm/plastic wrap.

My friend Greg Thomas makes the best leek tart. This is my gluten-free version, laden with butter and cream, so best to serve with a salad to counter the calories!

creamy leek tart

Begin by preparing the leeks as they need to cool before being used in the filling. Peel and slice the leeks into small rings. Put them in a saucepan with the butter and season with salt and pepper. Cook over a gentle heat for 15–20 minutes until soft and starting to caramelize but not brown. Set aside to cool.

To make the pastry, rub the butter into the flour using your fingertips, then add the salt and cheese and bring together into a soft ball of dough, adding 1–2 tablespoons water if the mixture is too dry. Wrap the dough in clingfilm/plastic wrap and chill in the refrigerator for 1 hour.

On a flour-dusted surface, roll out the pastry to 2–3 mm/⅛ inch thick and use it to line the tart pan. Press the pastry in firmly with your fingers and trim away any excess using a sharp knife. If the pastry breaks, don't worry, just patch any holes with the pastry trimmings. Prick the base and chill in the refrigerator for a further 30 minutes.

Preheat the oven to 180°C (350°F) Gas 4.

Line the pastry case with non-stick baking paper, fill with baking beans and bake for about 15–20 minutes until the pastry is golden brown. Remove the tart case from the oven and leave to cool slightly. Remove the baking paper and baking beans. Turn the oven temperature down to 120°C (250°F) Gas ½.

Spoon three-quarters of the cooled leeks into the pastry case (reserving a quarter of the leeks for the topping) and spread evenly. Whisk together the egg yolks and cream in a jug/pitcher and season with salt and pepper. Slowly pour the cream mixture over the leeks in the tart shell, then spoon the remaining leeks over the top of the tart. Carefully transfer the tart to the oven and bake for about 1½ hours until the top of the tart is lightly golden brown and set with a slight wobble in the centre. Leave to cool and then chill in the refrigerator until you are ready to serve.

The tart will keep for up to 3 days in the refrigerator in an airtight container or covered in clingfilm/plastic wrap.

For the pastry
80 g/5 tablespoons butter, chilled
180 g/1½ cups gluten-free plain/all-purpose flour, sifted, plus extra for dusting
½ teaspoon salt
100 g/1 cup grated Cheddar cheese

For the leek filling
800 g/1 lb. 12 oz. leeks
100 g/6½ tablespoons butter
6 egg yolks
350 ml/1½ cups double/heavy cream
sea salt and ground black pepper

a 25-cm/10-inch tart pan, greased
baking beans

Serves 8

Quiche Lorraine is a classic French tart; smoked bacon and onions surrounded by a rich and creamy egg custard. Although purists may object, I like to add sweetcorn and Cheddar cheese for extra flavour and texture, but you can omit these if you wish. This is a great lunch dish, ideal served with potato salad and green leaves.

quiche lorraine

For the pastry

90 g/6 tablespoons butter, chilled

190 g/1½ cups gluten-free plain/all-purpose flour, sifted, plus extra for dusting

1 egg yolk

1 tablespoon cream cheese

¼ teaspoon salt

1 teaspoon cracked black pepper

1–2 tablespoons milk (optional)

For the filling

1 large onion, finely sliced

1 tablespoon olive oil

240 g/9 oz. streaky/fatty bacon, cut into small strips

3 eggs, plus 2 egg yolks

300 ml/1¼ cups double/heavy cream

140 g (drained weight)/1 cup sweetcorn/corn kernels

60 g/a generous ½ cup grated Cheddar cheese

sea salt and ground black pepper

a 30 x 20-cm/12 x 8-inch loose-based tart pan, greased

baking beans

Serves 8

For the filling, put the sliced onion and olive oil in a frying pan and cook over a medium heat. Once the onion starts to soften, add the bacon to the pan and fry until the bacon is cooked and starts to turn light golden brown at the edges. Remove from the heat and leave to cool.

To make the pastry, rub the butter into the flour using your fingertips, then add the egg yolk, cream cheese, salt and pepper. Bring the dough together into a soft ball, adding 1–2 tablespoons milk if the mixture is too dry. Wrap the pastry dough in clingfilm/plastic wrap and chill in the refrigerator for 1 hour.

On a flour-dusted surface, roll out the pastry to a large rectangle just bigger than the size of the tart pan and use it to line the pan. Press the pastry in firmly with your fingers and trim away any excess using a sharp knife. If the pastry breaks, don't worry, just patch any holes with the pastry trimmings. Chill the pastry case in the refrigerator for 30 minutes.

Preheat the oven to 180°C (350°F) Gas 4.

Line the pastry case with non-stick baking paper, fill with baking beans and bake for about 15–20 minutes until the pastry is golden brown. Remove the tart case from the oven and leave to cool slightly. Remove the baking paper and baking beans. Turn the oven temperature down to 140°C (275°F) Gas 1.

Whisk together the eggs, egg yolks and cream, then stir in the onion and bacon, sweetcorn/corn and grated cheese and season with salt and pepper. Pour the mixture into the baked pastry case and bake the quiche for about 1½ hours until the filling is just set but still has a slight wobble in the centre. Leave to cool, then chill in the refrigerator until you are ready to serve.

The quiche will keep for up to 2 days in the refrigerator in an airtight container or covered in clingfilm/plastic wrap.

Although avocado is most often served cold in salads, it is delicious when baked. You need to ensure that it is thoroughly coated in lemon juice so that it does not discolour in the tart. This is a rich tart and is perfect to serve at Christmas with a glass of Prosecco or Champagne.

smoked salmon & avocado flan

To make the pastry, rub the butter into the flour using your fingertips, then mix in the lemon zest, salt, egg yolk and cream cheese. Bring together to a soft dough with your hands, adding 1–2 tablespoons milk if the mixture is too dry. Wrap the pastry dough in clingfilm/plastic wrap and chill in the refrigerator for 1 hour.

On a flour-dusted surface, roll out the pastry to a circle just bigger than the size of the tart pan and use it to line the pan, trimming away any excess using a sharp knife. If the pastry breaks, don't worry, just patch any holes with the pastry trimmings. Chill the pastry case in the refrigerator for 30 minutes.

Preheat the oven to 180°C (350°F) Gas 4.

Line the pastry case with non-stick baking paper, fill with baking beans and bake for about 15–20 minutes until the pastry is golden brown. Remove the tart case from the oven and leave to cool slightly. Remove the baking paper and baking beans. Turn the oven temperature down to 110°C (225°F) Gas ¼.

For the filling, peel the avocados and remove the pits. Cut them into thin slices and coat very well in the lemon juice to prevent them turning brown.

In a large mixing bowl, whisk together the egg yolks and cream, then add the avocado and lemon juice, and the salmon and season with pepper. (You do not need to add any salt as the smoked salmon is sufficiently salty.) Pour the mixture into the baked pastry case and bake for about 1½ hours until the filling is just set but still has a slight wobble in the centre. Leave to cool, then chill in the refrigerator until you are ready to serve.

The tart needs to be eaten on the day it is made as the avocado can discolour.

For the pastry
90 g/6 tablespoons butter, chilled and cubed
190 g/1½ cups gluten-free plain/all-purpose flour, sifted, plus extra for dusting
grated zest of 1 lemon
¼ teaspoon salt
1 egg yolk
1 tablespoon cream cheese
1–2 tablespoons milk (optional)

For the filling
2 small ripe avocados
freshly squeezed juice of 2 lemons
5 egg yolks
300 ml/1¼ cups double/heavy cream
180 g/6 oz. smoked salmon, cut into strips
freshly ground black pepper

a 25-cm/10-inch loose-based tart pan, greased
baking beans

Serves 8–10

Roasted tomatoes and creamy goats' cheese are a winning flavour combination. Encased in a tangy Parmesan pastry crust, these little tarts make a perfect snack. If you prefer, you can make miniature versions in tiny tart cases, topped with just one tomato.

roasted tomato tarts

For the pastry

90 g/6 tablespoons butter, chilled
190 g/1½ cups gluten-free plain/ all-purpose flour, sifted, plus extra for dusting
50 g/scant 1 cup grated Parmesan cheese

For the filling

600 g/1 lb. 5 oz. cherry tomatoes on the vine
4–5 sprigs of fresh thyme
2 tablespoons olive oil
1 tablespoon balsamic vinegar
½ tablespoon caster/granulated sugar
200 g/7 oz. creamy goats' cheese or other soft creamy cheese
sea salt and ground black pepper

8 x 10-cm/4-inch loose-based mini tart pans, greased
a pastry cutter slightly bigger than the tart pans
baking beans

Makes 8

To make the pastry, rub the butter into the flour using your fingertips, then mix in the grated Parmesan. Add a tablespoon of water and bring together to a soft dough with your hands, adding a further 1–2 tablespoons water if the mixture is too dry. Wrap the pastry dough in clingfilm/plastic wrap and chill in the refrigerator for 1 hour.

On a flour-dusted surface, roll out the pastry to 2–3 mm/⅛ inch thick and use the pastry cutter to stamp out circles of pastry just larger than the size of your tart pans. Line the pans with the pastry, pressing it in firmly with your fingertips and patching any cracks with the trimmings. Trim away any excess at the edges using a sharp knife. Prick the bases and chill in the refrigerator for a further 30 minutes.

Preheat the oven to 180°C (350°F) Gas 4.

Line the pastry cases with non-stick baking paper, fill with baking beans and bake them for 10–15 minutes until the pastry is golden brown. Leave to cool, but leave the oven on to cook the tomatoes. Once cool, remove the baking paper and baking beans.

Put the tomatoes in a roasting pan with the thyme sprigs and drizzle with the olive oil and balsamic vinegar. Sprinkle over the sugar and season with salt and black pepper. Bake for 15–20 minutes until the tomatoes have softened and are starting to caramelize. Remove from the oven and leave to cool.

Assemble the tarts just before serving. Place a generous spoonful of the cheese in the base of each tart case, top with the roasted tomatoes and short sprigs of the roasted thyme, drizzle with the roasting juices and serve.

The tart cases will keep, unfilled, for up to 3 days in an airtight container.

As an alternative to the popular French sweet dessert tatins, this is
a savoury version, packed with butternut squash and warming chilli.
It is delicious served warm accompanied by a creamy
Greek-style yogurt and a tangy dressed green salad.

butternut squash & chilli tatin

Preheat the oven to 180°C (350°F) Gas 4.
Cut the squash in half and remove the seeds
using a spoon, then cut it into 2-cm/1-inch thick slices,
leaving the skin on if you wish. Put the squash in a roasting
pan and drizzle with the olive oil. Add the thyme, garlic and
chillies to the pan, season with salt and pepper and roast for about 40
minutes until the squash is soft but still holds its shape and is starting to caramelize.
Remove from the oven and leave to cool slightly. If you are going to be cooking the
tart immediately, leave the oven on.

For the glaze, heat together the butter, sugar and vinegar in a small saucepan until
thin and syrupy, then pour it into the pan. Scatter the roasted chillies and thyme sprigs
on the base of the dish and arrange the roasted butternut squash slices in a pattern
on top.

To make the pastry, mix together the flour and suet/vegetable shortening and
season with salt and pepper. Add the milk gradually (you may not need it all
depending on the absorption rate of your flour, which differs from brand to brand)
and bring the mixture together into a soft dough.

Preheat the oven again to 180°C (350°F) Gas 4.

On a flour-dusted surface, roll out the dough to a circle just larger than the size of
the pan. Using a rolling pin, gently lift the pastry circle on top of the butternut squash
in the pan and press it down tightly. Patch any cracks with pastry trimmings. Bake the
tatin in the preheated oven for 20–25 minutes until the pastry is golden brown.
Remove from the oven, invert onto a serving plate and serve straight away.

For the squash
1 large butternut squash
80 ml/⅓ cup olive oil
5 sprigs thyme
2 garlic cloves, sliced
2 large red chillies, whole
sea salt and ground black pepper

For the glaze
30 g/2 tablespoons butter
1 tablespoon caster/granulated sugar
1 tablespoon balsamic vinegar

For the pastry
150 g/1 cup plus 2 tablespoons gluten-free plain/all-purpose flour, sifted, plus extra for dusting
90 g gluten-free shredded suet OR 6 tablespoons vegetable shortening, chilled and grated
sea salt and ground black pepper
about 120 ml/½ cup milk

a 20-cm/8-inch tatin pan or cast-iron frying pan/skillet, greased

Serves 4–6

This is a great pie to serve during the festive season, bursting with spices and cranberries and sweetened with a little apple purée. Hot crust pastry works really well in a gluten-free version and you would be able to serve this pie to anyone without them knowing it is gluten free.

apple & cranberry pork pie

For the pastry

300 g/2⅓ cups gluten-free plain/ all-purpose flour

2 teaspoons gluten-free Dijon mustard

1 teaspoon salt

140 g/generous ½ cup lard

For the filling

200 g smoked bacon lardons/ 1 cup thick-sliced back bacon cut into cubes

300 g/10½ oz. minced/ground pork

200 g/7 oz. fresh pork belly, rind trimmed and very finely chopped

1 teaspoon ground allspice

2 tablespoons apple sauce

sea salt and ground black pepper

For the topping

250 g/2 cups fresh cranberries

2 tablespoons redcurrant jelly

a 18-cm/7-inch round loose-based deep cake pan, greased

Serves 8

Preheat the oven to 180°C (350°F) Gas 4.

For the pastry, sift the flour into a large mixing bowl and add the mustard and salt. Heat the lard in a saucepan with 130 ml/½ cup water and bring to the boil, then carefully pour into the flour and beat in with a wooden spoon. Leave to cool for a few minutes, then, while the pastry is still warm, press the pastry into the base and sides of the cake pan evenly so that the pastry comes to the top of the pan sides. Press the edge into a fluted pattern with your fingertips.

In a bowl, mix together the bacon, minced/ground pork and pork belly with the allspice and apple sauce. Season well with salt and pepper and spoon the mixture into the pastry case, pressing in tightly with the back of a spoon, until the pastry case is full to just below the rim of the pastry (you may not need all of the meat). Cover the top of the meat with non-stick baking paper and press down firmly. Bake the pie in the preheated oven for 30 minutes, then turn the temperature down to 150°C (300°F) Gas 2 and bake for a further 2 hours until the juices from the meat run clear, then leave to cool.

For the topping, simmer the cranberries in 100 ml/scant ½ cup of water, seasoned with salt and pepper, until the cranberries are just soft and their skins start to split. Strain the water from the cranberries, leave them to cool slightly, then spoon the cranberries on top of the pie. Heat the redcurrant jelly in a saucepan with 1 tablespoon of water until the jelly has melted and is of a pourable consistency. Spoon over the cranberries and leave to cool.

The pie will store in the refrigerator for up to 3 days in an airtight container.

When the weather is cold, there is nothing nicer than tucking into a hearty pie straight from the oven. Beer usually contains gluten, but there is a good variety of gluten-free beers available, which work well in this recipe.

beef & ale pie

Preheat the oven to 180°C (350°F) Gas 4.

Heat half the oil in the casserole dish and add the onions and garlic. Season with salt and pepper and sauté over a gentle heat until they are soft and a light golden brown colour, then remove them from the pan. Add the remaining oil to the pan and, in batches, brown the meat on all sides, seasoning with salt and pepper. Remove the meat from the pan and drain off any oil. Add the meat, onions and garlic back to the pan along with the carrots, leek, mushrooms, beer and stock. Put the lid on the casserole and transfer it to the preheated oven to cook for about an hour, until the meat is tender.

Remove the pan from the oven and set it on the hob/stovetop to simmer. Remove a ladleful of the stock and stir in the cornflour/cornstarch. Pour it back into the pan and stir in, along with the brandy and creamed horseradish. Stir over the heat until the sauce starts to thicken, then pour into the pie dish and leave to cool.

For the pastry, mix together the flour, baking powder (plus xanthan gum, if using), suet/vegetable shortening and creamed horseradish in a large mixing bowl. Add the milk to the bowl gradually (you may not need it all depending on the absorption rate of your flour, which differs from brand to brand) and bring the mixture together with your hands to form a soft dough that is not sticky.

On a flour-dusted surface, roll out the pastry dough to a size slightly larger than your pie dish. Place a pie funnel in the middle of the filling in the dish and then cover the dish with the pastry, piercing a hole in the middle so that the pie funnel comes up through the pastry. Crimp the pastry with your fingers around the edge of the dish to seal. Decorate the pie top with any pastry trimmings cut out into the shape of leaves. Brush the top of the pie with beaten egg using a pastry brush and bake in the oven for about 25–30 minutes until the pastry crust is golden brown.

The pie is best eaten on the day it is made, although the filling can be made in advance and frozen for up to 1 month.

For the filling

2–3 tablespoons olive oil

1 onion, finely sliced

1 garlic clove, finely sliced

700 g/1½ lb. beef stewing steak

200 g/7 oz. baby carrots

1 leek, sliced and washed

200 g/7 oz. open cap mushrooms, quartered

500 ml/2 cups gluten-free beer

200 ml/¾ cup beef stock

1 tablespoon cornflour/cornstarch

60 ml/¼ cup brandy

1 tablespoon creamed horseradish

sea salt and ground black pepper

For the pastry

200 g gluten-free self-raising flour plus 2 teaspoons baking powder OR 1⅔ cups gluten-free all-purpose flour plus 3¾ teaspoons baking powder and 1¼ teaspoons xanthan gum, plus extra flour for dusting

110 g gluten-free shredded suet OR 7 tablespoons vegetable shortening, chilled and grated

1 tablespoon creamed horseradish

150–250 ml/⅔–1 cup milk

1 egg, beaten

a large flameproof lidded casserole

a 26-cm/10-inch diameter pie dish

a pie funnel

Serves 6

baked
dishes

This spicy chili is baked with a polenta topping flavoured with lime and coriander/cilantro for a real taste of Mexico. This is really a meal in itself and just needs a spoonful of sour cream and guacamole as an accompaniment. Make sure that the chilli bean sauce is gluten free.

chili polenta bake

Preheat the oven to 180°C (350°F) Gas 4.

Heat the olive oil in the saucepan set over a gentle heat, add the onion and garlic, season with salt and pepper and cook until lightly golden brown, adding a little water if the onion starts to brown too much. Remove the onion and garlic from the pan and set aside. Add a little further oil to the pan, add the beef and cook until it is browned. Once browned, remove from the pan and drain away any fat. Return the meat, onion and garlic to the pan and add the tomatoes, kidney beans and sauce, tomato purée/paste, brandy, chocolate and paprika and simmer for 10 minutes. Transfer the chilli to the baking dish and bake in the preheated oven for about 45 minutes, until the sauce is rich and thick. Remove the dish from the oven but leave the oven on.

For the topping, put the polenta in a saucepan along with 1 litre/4 cups water and simmer until the polenta is thick and has absorbed all the water (this should take about 3–5 minutes). Stir in the coriander/cilantro, lime zest and crème fraîche and season with salt and pepper.

Spoon the polenta over the top of the chilli, then sprinkle the grated cheese over the top. Bake in the oven for 25–30 minutes until the polenta crust is golden brown. Serve straight away with sour cream and guacamole.

For the chili
1–2 tablespoons olive oil
1 onion, finely chopped
1–2 garlic cloves, finely chopped
750 g/1 lb. 10 oz. lean minced/ ground beef
a 400-g/14-oz. can pomodorini tomatoes or chopped tomatoes
a 400-g/14-oz. can red kidney beans in chilli sauce
70 g/5 tablespoons tomato purée/paste
60 ml/¼ cup brandy
30 g/1 oz. dark chocolate, chopped
1 teaspoon hot smoked paprika
sea salt and ground black pepper

For the polenta crust
250 g/2 cups polenta express (pre-cooked maize meal)
2 tablespoons chopped fresh coriander/cilantro
grated zest of 1 lime
2 tablespoons crème fraîche or sour cream
80 g/¾ cup grated Cheddar cheese
sour cream, to serve
guacamole, to serve

an ovenproof baking dish

Serves 6–8

For the meat ragu

1–2 tablespoons olive oil

1 onion, finely chopped

1 garlic clove, finely chopped

1 carrot, peeled, trimmed and grated

750 g/1 lb. 10 oz. lean minced/ ground beef

200 g/¾ cup passata/crushed, strained tomatoes

a 400 g/14 oz. can chopped tomatoes

2 bay leaves

70 g/5 tablespoons double concentrate tomato purée/ paste

60 ml/¼ cup brandy

250 ml/1 cup red wine

125 ml/½ cup vegetable stock

For the cheese sauce

50 g/3½ tablespoons butter

1 tablespoon cornflour/cornstarch

500 ml/2 cups warm milk

200 g/2 cups grated Cheddar cheese

a pinch of grated nutmeg

sea salt and ground black pepper

For the pasta

115 g/scant 1 cup yellow cornflour/fine cornmeal

60 g/½ cup quinoa flour

3 eggs, beaten

½ teaspoon salt

gluten-free plain/all-purpose flour, for dusting

a flameproof lidded casserole

a large ovenproof baking dish

a silicone mat (optional)

Serves 6–8

This delicious lasagne uses a great basic gluten-free pasta recipe that is very useful to have in your repertoire.

lasagne

Preheat the oven to 180°C (350°F) Gas 4.

To make the meat ragu, heat the oil in the casserole pan and add the onion and garlic. Cook until the onion starts to turn a light golden brown and is soft, then add the carrot to the pan and continue to cook for a few minutes until the carrot starts to soften. Remove the onion, garlic and carrot from the pan and set aside. Add a little further oil to the pan and cook the beef in batches until it is browned. Remove from the pan and drain away any fat, then return the meat to the pan with the onion and carrot mixture. Add the passata, tomatoes, bay leaves, tomato purée/paste, brandy, red wine and stock and bring to the boil. Transfer the casserole to the oven and cook for about 1 hour until thickened. Remove any excess oil from the top with a spoon, then let cool.

For the cheese sauce, melt the butter in a saucepan and add the cornflour/cornmeal. Cook for a minute, then gradually add the warm milk, a little at a time, stirring continuously until you have a smooth sauce. Add three quarters of the cheese and stir until melted. Season with a little grated nutmeg, salt and pepper, then set aside until cool. Reserve the remaining cheese to sprinkle over the top of the lasagne.

Preheat the oven to 180°C (350°F) Gas 4. Set a pan of salted water to boil, ready to cook the pasta straight away. Spread half of the meat ragu over the base of your serving dish.

Sift together the yellow cornflour/cornmeal and quinoa flour, then tip it into a mound on a silicone mat or clean work surface. Make a well in the middle and add the eggs and salt. Mix the eggs into the flour with your fingertips until you have a soft dough.

Dust a work surface and a rolling pin with plenty of flour and cut the pasta dough into quarters. Coat liberally in flour and then roll out each quarter, one by one, very thinly. Once rolled out, cut the dough into rectangular sheets measuring about 15 x 8 cm/6 x 3½ inches. As soon as they are rolled out, cook the pasta sheets, one at a time for about 2 minutes. When cooked, remove each sheet from the water with a slotted spoon so that the water drains off and lay it on top of the meat. Repeat, rolling out and cooking enough pasta sheets to cover the bottom layer of meat. Cover the pasta with a layer of the cheese sauce and spread out thinly. Continue to roll out and cook more pasta sheets and layer them on top of the cheese sauce until it is completely covered. Spoon the remaining meat ragu on top of the pasta and spread out evenly. Cover with the remaining cheese sauce and top with the reserved grated cheese. Sprinkle a little nutmeg and cracked black pepper over the top of the lasagne, then bake in the preheated oven for about 30–40 minutes until the cheese is golden brown on top. Serve straight away or cook and then chill in the refrigerator for up to 2 days, reheating to serve.

This chicken crumble is delicious and makes a satisfying meal. If you are short of time, you can use ready-cooked chicken and good-quality bought chicken stock.

chicken & mushroom crumble

Put the wine, carrot, leek, onion, bay leaves and peppercorns in a large saucepan and add the whole chicken. Fill the pan with cold water so that the chicken is covered. Bring the liquid to the boil, the reduce the heat and leave to simmer for an hour until the chicken is cooked through. Remove the chicken from the pan and strain the stock, discarding the vegetables. Store the stock in the refrigerator until needed to cook the spinach.

Once cold, remove the chicken skin, cut away the chicken meat from the bones and chop it into bite-sized pieces. Discard the bones and skin and keep the chicken in the refrigerator until needed.

Preheat the oven to 180°C (350°F) Gas 4.

Melt the butter in a large saucepan, then add the mushrooms and spring onions/scallions and cook for about 3–5 minutes until soft. Add the cornflour/cornstarch to the pan and stir well. Cook over the heat for a few minutes then add the cream and 200 ml/¾ cup of the reserved chicken stock. Season with salt and pepper and simmer until the sauce thickens. Add the mustard and chicken to the pan and stir well so that everything is coated, then pour the mixture into the ovenproof dish.

In another saucepan, heat the remaining chicken stock then add the spinach and cook for 2–3 minutes until the spinach just starts to wilt. Drain and discard the stock (or cool and freeze for another day) and distribute the spinach in small spoonfuls evenly throughout the chicken mixture.

For the crumble topping, put the oats, flour (plus baking powder and xanthan gum, if using) and cornmeal in a bowl and rub the butter in with your fingertips until the mixture comes together in large lumps. Season with salt and pepper. Sprinkle the crumble over the creamy chicken filling so that it is evenly distributed, then bake in the preheated oven for 25–30 minutes until the crumble topping is golden brown. Serve straight away.

For the filling
250 ml/1 cup white wine

1 large carrot, peeled and chopped

1 leek, trimmed and sliced

1 onion, halved

2 bay leaves

1 teaspoon peppercorns

1 medium chicken (about 1.2 kg/ 2 lb. 10 oz.)

50 g/3½ tablespoons butter

250 g/9 oz. chestnut/cremini mushrooms, quartered

3 spring onions/scallions, finely chopped

2 tablespoons cornflour/cornstarch

400 ml/1⅔ cups double/heavy cream

1 tablespoon wholegrain mustard

100 g/3½ oz. spinach

sea salt and ground black pepper

For the crumble topping
120 g/1 cup gluten-free rolled oats

80 g gluten-free self-raising flour OR ⅔ cup gluten-free all-purpose flour plus ¾ teaspoon baking powder and ½ teaspoon xanthan gum

40 g/⅓ cup fine cornmeal

100 g/6½ tablespoons butter, chilled

an ovenproof baking dish

Serves 4

These delicate spinach and ricotta stuffed pancakes are inspired by my friend David Gibbs, who makes the best gluten-free pancakes ever.

crespolini

For the tomato sauce

120 ml/½ cup olive oil

1 onion, finely chopped

1 garlic clove, finely sliced

2 x 400 g/14 oz. cans plum tomatoes

sea salt and ground black pepper

For the béchamel sauce

50 g/3½ tablespoons butter

1 tablespoon cornflour/cornstarch

250 ml/1 cup milk

2 bay leaves

200 ml/¾ cup double/heavy cream

For the filling

250 g/9 oz. spinach

250 g/9 oz. ricotta

a pinch of freshly grated nutmeg

freshly squeezed juice of 1 lemon

1 teaspoon grated lemon zest

50 g/¾ cup grated Parmesan cheese, plus extra to sprinkle on top

For the pancakes

80 g/⅔ cup gluten-free plain/ all-purpose flour

2 eggs

1 teaspoon salt

butter, for frying

an ovenproof baking dish

Serves 3–4

To make the tomato sauce, heat the oil in a large saucepan, add the onion and garlic, season well with salt and pepper and cook for about 2–3 minutes.

Pour the tomatoes into a large bowl and squash them with your hands to break them into small pieces. Pour the tomatoes into the pan with the onions, taking care as the oil may spit as you pour them in, stir and leave to simmer for 2–2½ hours until the tomato sauce is thick and a deep rich colour. Leave to cool.

Next make the béchamel sauce. In a saucepan, melt the butter over a gentle heat, then add the cornflour/cornstarch and stir in well. Add the milk to the pan gradually, whisking all the time, then add the bay leaves. Cook for a few minutes until the sauce starts to thicken. Gradually add the cream and continue to stir over the heat until you have a smooth white sauce. Season with salt and pepper and set aside to cool. When cool, remove the bay leaves from the sauce.

For the filling, cook the spinach in salted boiling water for a few minutes, until the leaves just start to wilt but are still bright green. Strain, blanch in cold water, then strain again and firmly squeeze out all of the water. Finely chop the spinach with a sharp knife. Mix the spinach with the ricotta and season with salt and pepper, nutmeg and the lemon juice and zest, then fold in the Parmesan.

For the pancakes, whisk together the flour, eggs, salt and 200 ml/¾ cup water in a large mixing bowl until you have a thin batter. Heat a little butter in a frying pan, swirl it around to grease the pan, then pour off any excess butter. Add a ladleful of batter to the pan, swirling the pan as you pour the batter in to make sure that the whole base of the pan is coated in a thin layer. Once the batter is cooked through, turn the pancake over, either by flipping it (if you are brave!) or by using a spatula, and cook for a few minutes more on the other side. When cooked, transfer the pancake to a plate and repeat the process until all the batter is used, adding a little more butter to the pan each time, if necessary.

Preheat the oven to 180°C (350°F) Gas 4. Spoon a line of the ricotta mixture towards one end of a pancake, then roll it up. Repeat with the remaining pancakes until all the filling is used up. Spoon a few tablespoons of the tomato sauce into the baking dish and lay the pancakes in the dish. Spoon over more of the tomato sauce, then pour over the béchamel sauce. Sprinkle the top with a little grated Parmesan and black pepper and bake in the preheated oven for 20–25 minutes until the cheese turns golden brown. Serve straight away.

These individual pies, topped with fluffy mashed potato, are filled with filling root vegetables in a creamy white wine sauce.

golden vegetable pies

To make the filling, put the carrots, parsnips, swede/rutabaga, butter, bay leaves, wine and a little salt in a saucepan with enough water to cover the vegetables and simmer until the vegetables are soft but still hold their shape. Drain, remove the bay leaves, and leave to cool.

To make the pastry, rub the butter into the flour using your fingertips, then mix in the cream cheese, grated Cheddar and the salt and bring together into a soft ball of dough, adding 1–2 tablespoons water if the mixture is too dry. Wrap the pastry dough in clingfilm/plastic wrap and chill in the refrigerator for 1 hour.

Divide the dough into quarters. On a flour-dusted surface, roll out one portion of the pastry to 2–3 mm/⅛ inch thick and use it to line one of the pans. Press the pastry in firmly with your fingers and trim away any excess using a sharp knife. If the pastry breaks, don't worry, just patch any holes with the pastry trimmings. Repeat with the remaining pastry to line the remaining 3 pans. Prick the bases with a fork and chill in the refrigerator for a further 30 minutes.

Preheat the oven to 180°C (350°F) Gas 4.

Line the pastry cases with non-stick baking paper, fill with baking beans and bake them for about 15–20 minutes until the pastry is golden brown. Remove the pastry cases from the oven, leave for about 5 minutes to cool slightly, then remove the paper and baking beans and leave the tart cases in the pans to cool completely.

For the sauce, put the onion, wine and bay leaf in a saucepan and simmer over a gentle heat until the wine has reduced to about a quarter of the original volume of liquid. Add the stock and simmer again until the liquid has reduced by half. Add the cooked vegetables to the pan with the cream and mustard, then season well. Simmer for a few minutes until the sauce thickens slightly, then remove from the heat and leave to cool.

For the potato topping, boil the potatoes in salted water for about 20 minutes until they are soft. Remove from the heat, drain and pass through a sieve/strainer, pressing with the back of a spoon so that you have a smooth potato purée with no lumps. Whilst the potato is still hot, mix in the butter, milk and egg yolks, beating to make a smooth purée.

Preheat the oven again to 180°C (350°F) Gas 4. With the pastry cases still in the pans, fill each case with a few spoonfuls of the vegetable mixture and plenty of sauce until the pastry cases are almost filled. Spoon the potato purée over the top of the pies, smoothing with a round-bladed knife, then sprinkle each pie with a little grated Cheddar. Bake in the preheated oven for 20–25 minutes until the pies are golden brown on top. Carefully remove the pies from the pans, taking care as the pastry is fragile, and serve straight away.

For the vegetable filling

3 carrots, peeled and finely chopped

2 parsnips, peeled and finely chopped

1 swede/rutabaga, peeled and finely chopped

50 g/3½ tablespoons butter

2 bay leaves

125 ml/½ cup white wine

For the pastry

90 g/6 tablespoons butter, chilled

190 g/1½ cups gluten-free plain/all-purpose flour, sifted, plus extra for dusting

1 tablespoon cream cheese

60 g/generous ½ cup grated Cheddar cheese

¼ teaspoon salt

For the sauce

½ onion, finely chopped

250 ml/1 cup white wine

1 bay leaf

200 ml/¾ cup vegetable stock

150 ml/⅔ cup double/heavy cream

1 teaspoon gluten-free Dijon mustard

sea salt and ground black pepper

For the topping

550 g/1 lb. 4 oz. potatoes

80 g/5 tablespoons butter

120 ml/½ cup milk

2 egg yolks

3 tablespoons grated Cheddar cheese

4 x 13-cm/5-inch loose-based tart pans (3-cm/1-inch high), greased baking beans

Makes 4

This recipe was inspired by the wonderful chef Martin Lee at the Plough Restaurant in Bolnhurst, England. Gnudi are similar to gnocchi but are lighter as they are made without the potato. The gnudi can be prepared ahead of time and cooked shortly before serving. Baked with a light lemon sauce and Parmesan they are perfect served with a green salad.

gnudi bake

For the gnudi
500 g/1 lb. 2 oz. fresh spinach
250 g/9 oz. ricotta
freshly squeezed juice and grated
    zest of 1 lemon
a pinch of nutmeg
fine cornmeal, for dusting

For the sauce
freshly squeezed juice of
    2 lemons
50 g/3½ tablespoons butter
3 tablespoons grated Parmesan
    cheese
sea salt and ground black pepper

an ovenproof baking dish

Serves 2

Cook the spinach in boiling salted water for a few minutes until it is just wilted but still has a vibrant green colour. Drain, then plunge into cold water. When the spinach is cold, drain the water again and put the spinach in a clean dish towel and squeeze tightly to remove all the water. You need the spinach to be really dry so that the Gnudi are not soggy, so take the time to remove as much water as possible. Using a sharp knife, chop the spinach very finely and set aside.

In a large mixing bowl, mix the chopped spinach with the ricotta. Season with the lemon zest and juice, nutmeg and salt and pepper and mix well. Take small pieces of the mixture and roll it into balls the size of a walnut in your hands. Dust each gnudi lightly in the cornmeal as you go and place on a baking sheet. Continue until all the mixture is used up – it will make about 16 gnudi. Leave the gnudi to chill in the refrigerator for at least an hour.

When you are ready to serve, preheat the oven to 180°C (350°F) Gas 4.

Bring a saucepan of salted water to the boil, then turn it down to a simmer. Poach the gnudi for about 2 minutes (it is best to do this in batches), then remove them from the water with a slotted spoon, drain and place in the baking dish.

In a saucepan, heat the lemon juice and butter and stir until they have emulsified and become shiny. Season with salt and pepper. Pour the sauce over the gnudi and sprinkle with the grated Parmesan. Bake in the preheated oven for 3–5 minutes until the cheese has just melted. Serve straight away.

115

Whilst sweet cheesecakes are one of the world's best-loved desserts, this savoury recipe is just as delicious. Packed with slow roasted tomatoes, fresh basil and crumbly feta cheese, each slice offers a taste of the Mediterranean. It is however very rich, so you only need to serve small slices, accompanied by a dressed green salad.

sundried tomato & feta cheesecake

Preheat the oven to 180°C (350°F) Gas 4.

Put the tomatoes in a roasting pan, drizzle them with olive oil and sprinkle with the sugar, salt and pepper. Bake in the preheated oven for 20 minutes, then turn the temperature down to 140°C (275°F) Gas 1 and slow roast for a further hour. Remove from the oven and leave to cool in the pan.

Turn the oven up to 170°C (325°F) Gas 3.

Blitz the oatcakes to fine crumbs in a food processor or put them in a clean plastic bag and bash with a rolling pin. Transfer the crumbs to a large mixing bowl and stir in the melted butter. Tip the crumbs into the prepared cake pan and press them firmly into the base of the pan using the back of a spoon. Wrap the pan in clingfilm/plastic wrap and place in a large roasting pan half full of water, so that the water comes half way up the cheesecake pan.

For the filling, whisk together the crème fraîche, eggs, cream cheese and flour. Add half of the roasted tomatoes and their juices and oil from the pan to the cheese mixture, along with the chopped basil and the feta cheese. Fold in so that everything is evenly distributed and season with salt and pepper. Pour the mixture over the oatcake base.

Arrange the remaining tomatoes on top of the cheesecake, keeping some of them on the vine for decoration if you wish. Transfer the pan, in its water bath, to the preheated oven and bake for 1–1½ hours until golden brown on top and the cheesecake still has a slight wobble in the centre. Remove the cheesecake from the water and leave to cool, then transfer to the refrigerator to chill for at least 3 hours, or preferably overnight. The cheesecake will keep for up to 3 days in the refrigerator.

For the filling

600 g/1 lb. 5 oz. cherry vine tomatoes
olive oil, to drizzle
2 teaspoons caster/granulated sugar
600 ml/2½ cups crème fraîche
4 eggs
600 g/1 lb. 5 oz. cream cheese
2 tablespoons gluten-free plain/all-purpose flour, sifted
20 g/a large handful fresh basil, chopped
200 g/7 oz. feta cheese
sea salt and ground black pepper

For the base

250 g/9 oz. gluten-free oatcakes
125 g/1 stick butter, melted

a 25-cm/10-inch spring form cake pan, greased and lined

Serves 12

This pizza is unconventional as it contains no tomatoes, but with fragrant rosemary and crisp thin potato slices, it is no less satisfying than a regular pizza. It is a great accompaniment to serve with barbecued food in the summer, but is also delicious served with a simple salad.

potato & rosemary pizza

For the pizza base

150 ml/⅔ cup warm milk

1 tablespoon fast-action dried yeast

1 tablespoon caster sugar

300 g/2⅓ cups gluten-free strong white bread flour

1 teaspoon baking powder

1 teaspoon xanthan gum

1 teaspoon salt

1 egg

60 ml/¼ cup olive oil

80 ml/⅓ cup plain set yogurt

1 teaspoon finely chopped fresh rosemary

yellow cornflour/fine cornmeal or gluten-free flour, for dusting

For the topping

1 garlic clove, thinly sliced

60 ml/¼ cup olive oil

1 large potato

a few sprigs of fresh rosemary

sea salt and cracked black pepper

2 tablespoons grated Parmesan

a silicone mat (optional)

a large baking sheet

a mandolin (optional)

Serves 4

Put the warm milk, yeast and sugar in the jug/pitcher and leave in a warm place for about 10 minutes until the yeast has activated and a thick foam has formed on top of the liquid.

Sift the flour, baking powder and xanthan gum into a large mixing bowl and add the salt, egg, olive oil, yogurt, chopped rosemary and the yeast mixture. Stir everything together with a wooden spoon until well incorporated and you have a soft dough. Knead the dough a little with your hands and form it into a smooth ball, dusting with a little flour if the dough is too sticky.

Dust a sheet of baking paper or a silicone mat with a little cornflour/cornmeal. Roll out the dough thinly on the paper or mat to a large circle measuring about 30 cm/12 inches in diameter. Slide the dough onto a baking sheet, paper or silicone mat and all, and leave it in a warm place to prove for about 45–60 minutes until it becomes puffy. Preheat the oven to 190°C (375°F) Gas 5.

For the topping, put the garlic and olive oil in a saucepan set over a gentle heat and cook until the garlic turns lightly golden brown, then leave to cool. Once cool, use a pastry brush to brush the top of the pizza with some of the garlic-infused oil.

Slice the potato very thinly – this is best done on a mandolin. (You can peel the potato if you wish but I prefer to leave the skins on as they give a prettier pattern.) Lay the potato slices on top of the pizza, overlapping them slightly. Sprinkle with rosemary, sea salt and pepper and brush the top with more of the garlic oil. Sprinkle the pizza with the Parmesan and bake in the preheated oven for 20–25 minutes until the dough is crisp and the potatoes are cooked and golden brown. Serve straight away.

Calzone are Italian stuffed pizzas. You can vary the fillings – peppers, sun-dried tomatoes and cooked chicken in BBQ sauce all work well. Gluten-free pizza dough can be fragile, so take care when folding the calzone shape and only fill the calzone once the dough has proved.

calzone

Put the warm milk, yeast and sugar in a jug/pitcher and leave in a warm place for about 10 minutes until the yeast has activated and a thick foam has formed on top of the liquid.

Sift the flour, baking powder and xanthan gum into a large mixing bowl. Add the salt, egg, olive oil and yogurt and the yeast mixture, and stir together with a wooden spoon until everything is incorporated and you have a soft dough. Knead the dough a little with your hands and form it into a smooth ball, dusting with a little flour if the dough is too sticky.

Dust a sheet of baking paper or a silicone mat with a little cornflour/cornmeal. Roll out the dough thinly on the baking paper to a large circle measuring about 30 cm/12 inches in diameter. Slide the dough onto a baking sheet, paper or silicone mat and all, and leave it in a warm place to prove for about 45–60 minutes until it becomes puffy.

Preheat the oven to 180°C (350°F) Gas 4.

Spread the passata/crushed tomatoes over half of the dough leaving a small gap around the edge. Lay the mozzarella slices on top of the passata/crushed tomatoes and top with the salami, basil and sliced mushrooms. Wet the bare edges of the dough with a little water. Using the baking paper or silicone mat, lift the un-topped dough half over the filling so that the filling is completely covered and you have a semi-circle shaped calzone. Press the edges together tightly. As the gluten-free dough can be fragile a few cracks may appear on top of the dough, but do not worry as these will be covered by the cheese.

Sprinkle the grated mozzarella over the top of the calzone and bake in the preheated oven for 20–25 minutes until the dough is golden brown. Serve straight away.

For the pizza dough

150 ml/²⁄₃ cup warm milk

1 tablespoon fast-action dried yeast

1 tablespoon caster/granulated sugar

300 g/2¹⁄₃ cups gluten-free strong white bread flour, sifted

1 teaspoon baking powder

1 teaspoon xanthan gum

1 teaspoon salt

1 egg

60 ml/¼ cup olive oil

80 ml/¹⁄₃ cup plain set yogurt

yellow cornflour/fine cornmeal or gluten-free flour, for dusting

For the filling

100 g/scant 1 cup passata/crushed, strained tomatoes

125 g/4 oz. ball of mozzarella, sliced

50 g/2 oz. Napoli salami, cut into strips

1 tablespoon finely chopped fresh basil

30 g/1 oz. button mushrooms, finely sliced

For the topping

50 g/½ cup grated mozzarella

a silicone mat (optional)

Serves 4

party bites

These pastries are great to serve with sherry, and you can vary the cheese to any combination of hard cheeses you have in the fridge.

cheese straws

Cut half of butter into small cubes and rub it into the flour using your fingertips or a stand mixer. Add the lemon juice and xanthan gum and mix in. Stir in the cold water, a little at a time (you may not need it all), using a round bladed knife or a stand mixer until you have a soft dough. The dough should be soft but not sticky.

Grate the remaining half of the chilled butter on a coarse grater and keep it chilled until you need it, ideally in the freezer.

Lay a large piece of non-stick baking paper on a clean work surface and dust it with plenty of flour. Transfer the dough onto the baking paper and dust liberally with flour. Use a flour-dusted rolling pin to roll out the pastry to a large rectangle (about 50 x 18 cm/20 x 7 inches). Sprinkle half of the grated butter over the pastry and dust liberally with flour. With one of the shorter edges of the rectangle in front of you, fold the bottom third of the rectangle into the middle so that one third of the pastry is folded over the middle third of the pastry (use the baking paper to help you lift the pastry over). Press the folded pastry down with your hands. Next, take the top third of the pastry and fold it down carefully so it also lies over the middle third. Press down again with your hands. You should now be left with a rectangle measuring about one third of the size that it was.

Dust the surface and rolling pin with flour again, turn the pastry over and roll out into a 50 x 18-cm/20 x 7-inch rectangle again with the folds in the same direction as they were originally rolled (and not rotated as you would with traditional puff pastry). Sprinkle the rolled out pastry with the remaining grated butter, dust again with flour and repeat the folding steps.

Dust the surface and rolling pin again and repeat the rolling out stages twice more (this time without adding any butter but still dusting with flour), each time ensuring that the folds and the direction you are rolling out are the same as this helps the layers to rise. Trim any rough edges and your pastry is ready to use. For best results, use the pastry immediately and do not chill. Preheat the oven to 180°C (350°F) Gas 4.

On a flour-dusted surface, roll out the pastry to a rectangle about 2–3 mm/⅛ inch thick, then cut it into 20 rectangles measuring about 12 x 2 cm/5 x ¾ inch. Transfer them to the prepared baking sheet using a spatula. Mix together the grated Cheddar and Parmesan and sprinkle it over the pastry. Season with salt and pepper and bake in the preheated oven for 10–15 minutes until the pastry and cheese is golden brown. Leave the straws to cool on the baking sheet before serving.

For the pastry
200 g/1 stick plus 5 tablespoons butter, chilled
175 g/1⅓ cups gluten-free plain/all-purpose flour, sifted, plus extra for dusting
2 teaspoons lemon juice
1 teaspoon xanthan gum
60–80 ml/¼–⅓ cup ice cold water

For the topping
80 g/¾ cup finely grated Cheddar cheese
30 g/⅓ cup finely grated Parmesan cheese
sea salt and ground black pepper

a stand mixer (optional)
a large baking sheet, greased

Makes 20

Cheese and biscuits/crackers served with a tangy chutney make a great party snack. These ones, bursting with Cheddar cheese, are rich and buttery and melt in the mouth. And they are surprisingly quick and easy to prepare and will keep well stored in an airtight container, although they are quite fragile so do store them carefully.

cheese biscuits

170 g/1⅓ cups gluten-free plain/
all-purpose flour, plus extra for
dusting

115 g/1 stick butter, chilled and
cubed

100 g/1 cup grated Cheddar
cheese

a little milk (optional)

a 7.5-cm/3-inch round cookie
cutter

a large baking sheet, greased
and lined

Makes 15

Preheat the oven to 180°C (350°F) Gas 4.

Sift the flour into a large mixing bowl. Rub the butter into the flour with your fingertips until it resembles fine breadcrumbs. Add the cheese and mix together to form a soft dough, adding a little water or milk if the mixture is too dry. Wrap the dough in clingfilm/plastic wrap and chill in the refrigerator for 1 hour.

On a flour-dusted surface, roll out the dough to about 2–3 mm/⅛ inch thick and cut out 15 rounds using the cutter. Arrange the crackers on the baking sheet and bake in the preheated oven for 10–15 minutes until golden brown. Leave to cool on the baking sheet before serving.

These tasty cheese pastry tartlets, filled with sweet and sour caramelized onions and a slice of melted Brie, make great canapés. If you prefer, you can make 6 larger tarts in 12-cm/5-inch tart tins/pans, which are the perfect size for an appetizer or light lunch. Top with fresh thyme or thyme flowers if you have them in your garden.

brie & caramelized onion tartlets

To make the pastry, put both the flours in a food processor. Add the butter and cheese and blitz until the mixture resembles fine breadcrumbs. Tip into a bowl and add the egg yolk, buttermilk and mustard and mix together to form a soft dough. If the dough is too dry add a little water and if it is too sticky add a little extra flour. Form the dough into a ball, wrap in clingfilm/plastic wrap and chill for 1 hour.

Preheat the oven to 180°C (350°F) Gas 4. Dust a work surface with flour and use a rolling pin to roll out the pastry to a thickness of 3 mm/⅛ inch. Stamp out 16 rounds using the cutter and press them into the holes in the prepared tin/pan. Line each pastry case with baking parchment, fill with baking beans and bake in the preheated oven for 10–15 minutes, until the pastry is crisp and golden.

Meanwhile, make the onion filling. Put the onions in a large frying pan/skillet with the butter and oil. Season and cook over gentle heat, until the onions are caramelized and golden brown, adding a little water if the onions start to brown too much. Add the vinegar, sugar and allspice and cook until the sugar has dissolved and the onions are sticky. Let cool, then put a spoonful of onions in each pastry case. Cut the brie into 16 pieces of equal size and put a slice on top of each tartlet and sprinkle with sprigs of thyme. Bake in the oven at 180°C (350°F) Gas 4 for about 5–10 minute, until the cheese starts to melt. Remove the tartlets from the tins/pans, season with black pepper and serve warm or cold.

These tartlets are best eaten on the day they are made.

3 red onions, thinly sliced (about 350 g/12 oz)

30 g/2 tablespoons butter

1 tablespoon olive oil

2 tablespoons balsamic vinegar

40 g/scant ¼ cup caster/ granulated sugar

1 teaspoon ground allspice

150 g/5½ oz brie

a few sprigs of fresh thyme

sea salt and freshly ground black pepper

For the cheese pastry

60 g/½ cup gluten-free plain/ all-purpose baking flour, sifted, plus extra for dusting

30 g/½ cup chestnut flour, sifted

40 g/3 tablespoons butter, chilled

70 g/½ cup grated Cheddar

1 egg yolk

1 tablespoon buttermilk

1 teaspoon mustard

2 x 12-hole mini tartlet tins/pans, greased with butter

baking beans

an 8-cm/3-inch round cutter

Makes 16 tartlets

These small flaky pastry bites make a simple but impressive canapé, topped with roasted tomatoes, mozzarella pearls and fresh basil. As an alternative you could top the tarts with slices of jarred roasted peppers in place of the tomatoes with equally delicious results.

mozzarella & tomato puffs

200 g/1 stick plus 5 tablespoons
   butter, chilled
175 g/1⅓ cups gluten-free plain/
   all-purpose flour, sifted, plus
   extra for dusting
2 teaspoons lemon juice
1 teaspoon xanthan gum
60–80 ml/¼–⅓ cup ice cold
   water

To assemble
5 tablespoons pesto
16 small cherry tomatoes
32 mozzarella pearls
fresh basil leaves
extra virgin olive oil, for drizzling
sea salt and ground black pepper

a stand mixer (optional)
8-cm/3½-inch and 6-cm/2½-inch
round cookie cutters
a large baking sheet, greased
and lined

Makes 16

Preheat the oven to 180°C (350°F) Gas 4.

Prepare the pastry according to the instructions for Cheese Straws on page 124, following the method for folding and refolding the pastry, until you reach the point where the pastry is rolled out.

On a flour-dusted surface, roll out the pastry to a rectangle about 2–3 mm/⅛ inch thick. Stamp out 16 rounds with the large pastry cutter and transfer them carefully to the prepared baking sheet.

Using the small cutter, imprint a smaller circle into centre of each pastry round, but do not cut all the way through. Spoon about a teaspoon of pesto into the centre of each pastry round.

Cut the cherry tomatoes in half and place two halves on top of each pastry round, together with two mozzarella pearls. Season with salt and pepper. Bake the puffs in the preheated oven for 10–15 minutes until the pastry is golden brown and the cheese and tomatoes are soft. Sprinkle with basil leaves and drizzle with a little olive oil, to serve.

131

The ingredients for these sausage rolls may seem a little unusual but you will have to trust me that the curry spices and mango chutney make them delicious. Topped with onion seeds for added flavour, these are great served with an Indian yogurt and mint raita dip.

spicy sausage rolls

To make the pastry, put the flour, butter and cream cheese in a food processor and blitz until the mixture resembles fine breadcrumbs. Tip into a large mixing bowl and add the egg yolk and mustard, then mix together with your hands to form a soft dough. If the mixture is too dry, add a little water and if it is too sticky, add a little extra flour. Form the dough into a ball, wrap it in clingfilm/plastic wrap and chill in the refrigerator for 1 hour.

To prepare the filling, remove the sausages from their skins and discard the skins. Mix the sausagemeat with the mango chutney and curry powder. Season with salt and pepper, cover with clingfilm/plastic wrap and chill in the refrigerator until needed.

Preheat the oven to 180°C (350°F) Gas 4.

Divide the chilled pastry into 2 portions. On a flour-dusted surface, roll out each portion to a rectangle measuring about 30 x 18 cm/12 x 7 inches and 2 mm/⅛ inch thick. Divide the sausage mixture in two and shape each portion into a long sausage. Take one of the pastry rectangles and place the sausage mixture down the centre of the long length. Wet both long edges of the rectangle with a little water and fold one of the halves over the sausagemeat so that it meets the pastry edge on the other side. Press down with your fingertips to seal in the sausagemeat. Trim any excess pastry from the long edge with a sharp knife and crimp with a fork. Cut the slice into 6 sausage rolls, then place them on the prepared baking sheet. Repeat with the other pastry rectangle and the remaining sausagemeat. Brush the top of each sausage roll with egg and sprinkle with onion seeds. Bake in the preheated oven for 25–30 minutes until the pastry is golden brown and the sausagemeat is cooked through.

You can eat these hot or cold and they will keep for up to 3 days in an airtight container in the refrigerator.

For the pastry
180 g/1½ cups gluten-free plain/all-purpose flour, sifted, plus extra for dusting
80 g/5 tablespoons butter, chilled
1 tablespoon cream cheese
1 egg yolk
1 teaspoon gluten-free Dijon mustard

For the filling
400 g/14 oz. gluten-free pork sausages
1 tablespoon mango chutney
1–2 teaspoons hot curry powder
sea salt and ground black pepper

To glaze
1 egg, beaten
black onion (nigella) seeds, for sprinkling

a baking sheet, greased and lined

Makes 12

These light choux buns are great to serve as canapés. Filled with a goats' cheese cream and topped with crispy bacon, they are truly delicious. Once you have mastered choux pastry, you can vary the fillings – prawn/shrimp and avocado mousse, smoked salmon and cream cheese, creamy mushrooms – the possibilities are endless!

cheese & bacon choux buns

For the buns

65 g/½ cup gluten-free plain/all-purpose flour

50 g/3½ tablespoons butter

2 large eggs

30 g/⅓ cup finely grated Emmenthal cheese

25 g/1 oz. crispy cooked smoked bacon, finely chopped

For the filling

150 g/5½ oz. soft goats' cheese

300 ml/1¼ cups double/heavy cream

sea salt and ground black pepper

1 tablespoon snipped chives

a baking sheet, greased and lined

2 piping bags fitted with large round nozzles/tips

Makes 20

Preheat the oven to 200°C (400°F) Gas 6.

Sift the flour twice to remove any lumps. Heat the butter in a saucepan with 150 ml/⅔ cup water until the butter is melted, then bring to the boil. Add all the flour quickly and remove the pan from the heat. Beat hard with a wooden spoon until the dough forms a ball and no longer sticks to the sides of the pan. Leave to cool for about 5 minutes. Whisk the eggs, then beat them into the flour mixture, a little amount at a time, using a balloon whisk. The mixture will form a sticky paste which holds its shape when you lift the whisk up.

Spoon the batter into one of the piping bags and pipe 20 balls of choux pastry onto the prepared baking sheet. With clean hands, wet your finger and smooth down any peaks from the piping so that the pastry is smooth. Sprinkle the tops of the buns with the grated cheese and bacon bits, then bake in the preheated oven for 12–15 minutes. Remove from the oven and use a sharp knife to cut a small slit in each bun to allow the steam to escape, then return the buns to the oven for about 5 minutes until crisp. Leave to cool on a wire rack, then cut the buns in half.

For the filling, whisk together the goats' cheese and cream until the mixture comes into soft peaks. Season well with salt and pepper, then fold through the snipped chives. Spoon the mixture into the other piping bag and pipe a little of the cheese mixture into each choux bun. Serve straight away once filled.

These tartlets are the perfect smart canapé to serve with a glass of Champagne. Samphire is a green sea shrub which is great with any fish and I've paired it here with a smoked salmon mousse and quails' eggs. If you can't find samphire, they are delicious with watercress, too.

samphire & salmon tartlets

Begin by soft boiling the quails' eggs. Bring a pan of water to the boil and gently lower the eggs in. Cook for 2½ minutes then drain the eggs and submerge in cold water to stop them cooking. Once cool, peel the eggs and set aside.

To make the pastry, mix the flour and cornmeal together in a large mixing bowl. Rub the butter into the flour mixture with your fingertips until the mixture resembles fine breadcrumbs. Mix in the cream cheese, egg yolk and lemon zest and bring the mixture together into a ball, adding 1–2 tablespoons water if the mixture is too dry. Wrap the pastry in clingfilm/plastic wrap and chill in the refrigerator for 30 minutes. Preheat the oven to 180°C (350°F) Gas 4.

On a flour-dusted surface, roll out the pastry to 2–3 mm/⅛ inch thick and cut out 12 circles using the cutter, re-rolling the pastry as needed. Line each hole of the bun pan with a circle of pastry and press in lightly with your finger tips. Patch any cracks using the pastry trimmings. Line each case with a small piece of baking paper and fill with baking beans. Bake in the preheated oven for 8–12 minutes until crisp and golden brown. Leave to cool, then remove the baking beans and baking paper.

For the mousse, put the salmon in a food processor with the lemon and a little freshly ground black pepper and blitz until the salmon is finely chopped. Add the cream and blitz again until the cream thickens and you have a smooth mousse. Store in the refrigerator until you are ready to serve.

Blanche the samphire in boiling water for about 3 minutes, then plunge into iced water so that it retains its colour. Cut the soft-boiled quails' eggs in half.

To assemble, spoon the mousse into the piping bag and pipe a star into each pastry case. If you are not using a piping bag, place a spoonful of the mousse into each case. Lay a few samphire strands on top of the mousse. Cut the reserved smoked salmon into strips and place one on top of each tart, along with half a quails' egg to decorate. Season with a little cracked black pepper and serve straight away.

For the pastry

90 g/¾ cup gluten-free plain/all-purpose flour, sifted, plus extra for dusting

40 g/⅓ cup fine cornmeal

50 g/3½ tablespoons butter, chilled and cubed

1 tablespoon cream cheese

1 egg yolk

grated zest of 1 lemon

For the salmon mousse

100 g/3½ oz. smoked salmon

freshly squeezed juice of 1 lemon

freshly ground black pepper

150 ml/⅔ cup double/heavy cream

To assemble

50 g/2 oz. samphire or watercress

2 slices smoked salmon

6 quails' eggs

freshly cracked black pepper

a 12-hole mini tartlet pan, greased

an 8-cm/3-inch round fluted cutter

12 small squares of baking paper

baking beans

a piping bag fitted with large star nozzle/tip (optional)

Makes 12

breads
& doughs

Soda bread is traditionally from Ireland and is very quick and easy to prepare. It contains no yeast as the recipe uses bicarbonate of soda/baking soda to make it rise. It is great to serve with soups and casseroles. Cutting the cross on top of the loaf is important as it allows it to cook all the way through.

soda bread

Preheat the oven to 180°C (350°F) Gas 4.

Put the bread and oat flours in a large mixing bowl and add the bicarbonate of soda/baking soda and the salt. Add the buttermilk and milk and mix to form a soft dough. If it is too sticky, add a little more flour but don't overwork the dough – as there is no yeast, you need to keep the mixture as light as possible.

Form the dough into a round mound, about 4 cm/1½ inches high and 20 cm/8 inches in diameter. Cut a cross on the top of the loaf with a sharp knife and dust the top with a little extra flour. Put the loaf on the prepared baking sheet and bake in the preheated oven for 45–55 minutes until the bread is crusty on top and makes a hollow sound when tapped.

The bread is best eaten on the day you make it, but can be reheated in the oven the following day.

350 g/2¾ cups gluten-free strong brown bread flour, plus extra for dusting
200 g/1½ cups oat flour*
1 teaspoon bicarbonate of soda/baking soda
1 teaspoon salt
500 g/2 cups buttermilk
80 ml/⅓ cup milk

a baking sheet, greased

Makes 1 loaf

*Oat flour is available in health food shops and online, but if you cannot find it substitute gluten-free plain/all-purpose flour instead.

This delicious Italian focaccia bread is perfect eaten in summer. It is topped with fresh seasonal ingredients – juicy tomatoes, perfumed sprigs of fresh rosemary and olives.

rosemary, olive & tomato focaccia

2 teaspoons fresh yeast

2 teaspoons honey

2 tablespoons warm water

450 g gluten-free white bread flour OR 3½ cups gluten-free all-purpose baking flour plus 1½ teaspoons xanthan gum

300 ml/1 cup plus 3 tablespoons warm milk

2 eggs, beaten

1 teaspoon vinegar

3 tablespoons buttermilk

1 teaspoon fine sea salt

20 cherry tomatoes, halved

20 pitted black olives, halved

sprigs of fresh rosemary

olive oil, for drizzling

sea salt flakes

a 33 x 23-cm/13 x 9-inch shallow-sided baking tin/pan, greased with olive oil

Makes 1 large loaf

Put the yeast, honey and warm water in a cup and leave for 10–15 minutes, until the mixture becomes foamy.

Sift the flour into a mixing bowl and add the yeast mixture, warm milk, eggs, vinegar, buttermilk and fine salt and whisk together until everything is incorporated. Spoon the mixture into the prepared tin/pan, cover with a clean, damp kitchen towel and leave in a warm place for 1 hour, until the dough has doubled in size and risen.

When the dough has risen, preheat the oven to 190°C (375°F) Gas 5. Press the tomatoes, olives and rosemary into the top of the mixture, drizzle with olive oil and sprinkle with sea salt flakes. Bake in the preheated oven for about 30–40 minutes, until the bread springs back to the touch and has a crusty top.

This bread is best eaten warm on the day it is made.

Making gluten-free bread dough is very different to making regular bread dough. The steps to creating this tasty loaf couldn't be simpler as it requires no kneading and no proving. This bread keeps well if stored in an airtight container and makes delicious ham and mustard sandwiches. You can also substitute other flavours in place of the cheese and onion seeds if you prefer.

crusty cheese & onion bread

Preheat the oven to 180°C (350°F) Gas 4.

Sift the flour and baking powder into a mixing bowl. Add the eggs, melted butter and buttermilk. Fold in the Gruyère and Cheddar, together with the onion seeds and chives, until everything is mixed together well.

Spoon the mixture into the prepared tin/pan – the mixture will be quite sticky and resemble cake batter rather than traditional bread dough.

Sprinkle the Parmesan over the top and bake in the preheated oven for 40–50 minutes, until the top of the loaf is golden and springs back to your touch. Let cool in the tin/pan for about 5 minutes before turning out onto a wire rack to cool completely.

This bread will keep for up to 3 days if stored in an airtight container.

250 g gluten-free self-raising flour plus 3 teaspoons baking powder OR 2 scant cups gluten-free all-purpose flour plus 4 teaspoons baking powder and ½ teaspoon xanthan gum

3 eggs, beaten

50 g/3½ tablespoons butter, melted and cooled

280 ml/1 cup plus 2 tablespoons buttermilk

60 g/generous ½ cup grated Gruyère

60 g/generous ½ cup grated Cheddar

1 tablespoon black onion seeds

1 tablespoon snipped chives

3 tablespoons finely grated Parmesan

a 23-cm/9-inch springform cake tin/pan, greased and lined

Makes 1 round loaf

This fiery cornbread with a gooey cheese topping is a satisfying snack. Served still-warm from the oven, is the ideal accompaniment to chili con carne but is equally tasty eaten just on its own.

cheesy chilli cornbread

For the cornbread

100 g gluten-free self-raising flour plus 1 teaspoon baking powder OR ¾ cup gluten-free all-purpose flour plus 2 teaspoons baking powder and ½ teaspoon xanthan gum

300 g/2 cups fine cornmeal

2 teaspoons bicarbonate of soda/baking soda

4 tablespoons chopped fresh coriander/cilantro

grated zest of 1 lime

3 spring onions/scallions finely chopped

500 ml/2 cups buttermilk

50 g/3½ tablespoons butter, melted and cooled

3 eggs

sea salt and ground black pepper

For the cheesy chilli topping

2–3 red chillies, finely sliced

1 tablespoon olive oil

1 tablespoon finely chopped coriander/cilantro

2 teaspoons caster/granulated sugar

100 g/1 cup grated Cheddar cheese

a 25-cm/9-inch square baking tin/pan, greased and lined

Makes 1 large loaf

Begin by preparing the topping. Fry the chillies in a saucepan with the olive oil until soft. Season with salt and pepper, add the chopped coriander/cilantro and cook for a few minutes further. Sprinkle over the sugar and cook for a further minute until the chillies start to caramelize, then leave to cool.

Preheat the oven to 190°C (375°F).

Sift the flour and baking powder (plus xantham gum, if using) into a large mixing bowl and stir in the cornmeal, bicarbonate of soda/baking soda, coriander/cilantro, lime zest and spring onions/scallions.

In a separate bowl, whisk together the buttermilk, melted butter and eggs and season well with salt and pepper. Add this to the dry ingredients and mix everything together.

Pour the mixture into the prepared baking tin/pan and spread level using a spatula. Sprinkle the grated cheese over the top of the batter, then evenly distribute the chillies. Bake in the preheated oven for 30–35 minutes until the loaf is golden brown on top.

The bread is best served warm on the day it is made.

This is a dense loaf with a rich parsnip flavour. Parsnips are my favourite vegetable so, for me, this bread is irresistible! It is great for serving with soups and roasted meat, but does not keep well so needs to be eaten while fresh on the day it is made.

parsnip & rosemary bread

Bring a saucepan of salted water to the boil, add the parsnips and cook for about 20 minutes until soft. Drain the parsnips, then mash them with the butter using a potato masher to a smooth purée. Season with black pepper and set aside to cool.

Put the warm water in a jug/pitcher with the yeast and the sugar and leave in a warm place for about 10 minutes, until a thick foam has formed on top of the liquid.

Sift the flour and xanthan gum into the bowl of a stand mixer and stir in the salt and rosemary. Pour in the yeast mixture, add the parsnip purée and mix with a dough hook for 1–2 minutes. Add the oil and a little more warm water (about 50–100 ml/ 3–6 tablespoons), if needed, and mix again until you have a smooth dough.

Dust your hands with flour and bring the dough together into a ball. Place the dough on the prepared baking sheet. Cover with a clean damp cloth and leave to prove for 1½ hours, until the dough has doubled in size.

Preheat the oven to 180°C (350°F) Gas 4.

Brush the top of the loaf with the beaten egg and poke a few rosemary sprigs into the loaf to decorate. Sprinkle the top of the loaf with sea salt flakes, then bake the bread in the preheated oven for 35–45 minutes until golden brown and the loaf sounds hollow when you tap it. Serve warm with butter.

500 g/1 lb. parsnips, peeled and cut into chunks

1 tablespoon butter

100 ml/6½ tablespoons warm water, plus more, if required

7 g/1 envelope fast-action dried yeast

1 tablespoon caster/granulated sugar

550 g/4½ cups gluten-free strong white bread flour, plus extra for dusting

1 teaspoon xanthan gum

1 teaspoon salt

1 tablespoon fresh rosemary, finely chopped

40 ml/3 tablespoons olive oil

1 egg, beaten, to glaze

rosemary sprigs

sea salt flakes and ground black pepper

a stand mixer fitted with a dough hook

a large baking sheet, greased and lined

Makes 1 loaf

What gives a classic bagel its chewy texture and shiny coat is boiling it in water prior to baking. Unfortunately, given the fragile nature of gluten-free dough, this method just results in disintegration – bye bye bagel! I found the solution is to just submerge the bagels in boiling water, allowing them to float for a few seconds. The resulting bagels have a good chewy texture and are delicious toasted or filled.

onion seed bagels

150–200 ml/²⁄₃–¾ cup warm water

1 tablespoon gluten-free fast-action dried yeast

1 tablespoon white caster/granulated sugar

450 g/3½ cups gluten-free plain/all-purpose baking flour

2 whole eggs plus 1 whisked egg white

1 tablespoon black onion seeds, plus extra for sprinkling

2 tablespoons plain yogurt

2 baking sheets, lined

Makes 10

Put the warm water, yeast and sugar in a bowl and leave for 5–10 minutes, until the mixture is foamy. Sift the flour into a mixing bowl and add the 2 whole eggs. Pour in the yeast mixture and add the onion seeds and yogurt. Mix with your hands to form a soft, moist dough.

Divide the dough into 10 pieces of equal size and roll them into small balls. Press your thumb into the middle of the ball to make the bagel hole, smoothing the edges with your finger and using extra flour if the dough is too sticky to work. Arrange them a distance apart on the prepared baking sheets, cover with oiled clingfilm/plastic wrap and leave in a warm place for 1 hour.

Preheat the oven to 180°C (350°F) Gas 4. Fill a roasting tin/pan with boiling water and carefully transfer it to the bottom of the oven – this will create steam. Fill a large, deep heatproof dish with boiling water. Put a bagel on a slotted spoon and lower it into the water for about 10 seconds, until the bagel lifts off the spoon and floats. Use the spoon to remove it from the water and return it to the baking sheet. Repeat with the remaining bagels. When all the bagels have been in the water, brush them with a little egg white and sprinkle with onion seeds. Bake in the preheated oven for 20–30 minutes, until golden brown on top and underneath.

These bagels are best eaten on the day they are made.

Variation For breakfast cinnamon and raisin bagels, replace the onion seeds with 2 teaspoons cinnamon and 100 g/²⁄₃ cup raisins. When the bagels are brushed with egg white, sprinkle with caster/superfine sugar mixed with more cinnamon.

151

These flatbreads are ideal to serve cut into slices with dips in place of a pitta bread, or two of them can be filled with grated cheese and grilled for the perfect cheese melt. You can also add a variety of spices or herbs to the dough – finely chopped rosemary and thyme or Indian spices if you are serving as an accompaniment to curries and dhals.

flatbreads

Sift the plain/all-purpose flour into a mixing bowl and add the gram flour and salt. Pour in the oil and yogurt then add 60–80 ml/¼–⅓ cup water gradually, mixing with your hands until you have a ball of dough – you may not need all of the water. The dough should not be sticky at all and should be firmer than normal bread dough.

Divide the dough into 8 balls of equal size (about the size of a golf ball). Put them on a floured work surface and use a rolling pin to roll each ball out to a thin 20-cm/8-inches round.

Heat a dry frying pan/skillet until hot. Cook the breads one at a time for 2–3 minutes on one side then turn over and cook for a further 1–2 minutes on the other side, until lightly golden brown. If you wish, add a little oil to the pan towards the end of cooking so that the breads are lightly fried, which adds to the taste. For best cooking results, press down on the breads during cooking with a clean heatproof towel, which squeezes out the air and causes the breads to puff up slightly.

These breads are best eaten on the day they are made.

Variation To make spiced flatbreads add ½ teaspoon ground chilli, 1 teaspoon ground cumin and 1 teaspoon ground coriander, or 1 teaspoon garam masala or medium curry powder to the dough. Check that your spices do not contain any gluten before using.

200 g/1⅔ cups gluten-free plain/all-purpose baking flour

100 g/1⅓ cups gram (chickpea) flour

1 teaspoon fine sea salt

1 tablespoon sunflower or vegetable oil, plus extra for cooking (optional)

1 generous tablespoon plain yogurt

Makes 8 flatbreads

This is a delicious, slightly sweet focaccia bread, topped with crunchy nuts and plump, juicy raisins that have been soaked in sherry. It makes a great accompaniment to all sorts of soups and salads, or enjoyed on its own as a snack. It is best served warm on the day it is made.

walnut & raisin focaccia

100 g/⅔ cup raisins

125 ml/½ cup sherry

7 g/1 envelope fast-action dried yeast

1 tablespoon caster/granulated sugar

80 ml/⅓ cup warm water

450 g/3½ cups gluten-free strong white bread flour

250 ml/1 cup warm milk

2 eggs, beaten

1 teaspoon balsamic vinegar

1 teaspoon salt

100 g/⅔ cup walnut halves

a few sprigs of fresh rosemary

olive oil, for drizzling

sea salt flakes

a 33 x 23-cm/13 x 9-inch shallow-sided baking pan, greased with olive oil

Makes 1 large loaf

Begin by soaking the raisins in the sherry for about 3 hours until the fruit has plumped up.

Put the yeast, sugar and warm water in a jug/pitcher and leave in a warm place for about 10 minutes until a thick foam forms on top of the liquid.

Sift the flour into a large mixing bowl and add the yeast mixture, warm milk, eggs, vinegar and salt and whisk together until everything is incorporated. Spoon the mixture into the baking pan, cover with a damp tea/dish towel and leave in a warm place for 1 hour until the dough has doubled in size and risen.

Preheat the oven to 190°C (375°F) Gas 5.

Drain the raisins and sprinkle them over the dough, along with the walnuts. Poke small sprigs of rosemary into the dough at regular intervals. Drizzle the loaf generously with olive oil and sprinkle with sea salt. Bake in the preheated oven for 35–40 minutes until the bread springs back to the touch and has a crusty top. Serve warm or cold.

The focaccia is best eaten on the day it is made.

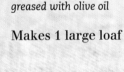

These delicious Indian breads are a perfect accompaniment to curries and other spiced dishes. Mine are flavoured with black onion seeds but you can add other flavourings of your choosing, such as a little garlic or finely chopped coriander/cilantro.

naan bread

Put the warm milk, yeast and sugar in a jug/pitcher and leave in a warm place for about 10 minutes until a thick foam has formed on top of the liquid.

Sift the flour, baking powder and xanthan gum into a large mixing bowl. Add the salt, egg, yogurt, melted ghee and onion seeds and the yeast mixture and mix well with a wooden spoon until everything is incorporated and you have a soft dough. Divide the dough into 6 portions.

Dust a clean surface generously with yellow cornflour/cornmeal and roll out each portion of dough into an oval shape, dusting the rolling pin with yellow cornflour/cornmeal, too, so that the bread does not stick. Place the rolled out naan breads onto the prepared baking sheets and leave in a warm place for about 45 minutes–1 hour until the naan have risen and are slightly puffy.

Preheat the oven to 200°C (400°F) Gas 6 and place the baking sheets inside. Heat the baking sheets for 5 minutes until they are very hot. Carefully place the naan breads on the baking sheets and cook for 4–5 minutes (you may find it easiest to do this in batches).

Remove the bread from the oven and heat a wok or large frying pan until very hot on the hob/stovetop. Add the naan breads to the pan, one at a time, and cook for a few minutes on each side until the naan have their classic brown spots. (You do not need to add any oil to the pan.) Brush the extra melted ghee over the top of the naan using a pastry brush, if you wish, and serve straight away.

150 ml/⅔ cup warm milk

1 tablespoon fast-action dried yeast

1 tablespoon caster/granulated sugar

300 g/2⅓ cups gluten-free strong white bread flour

1 teaspoon baking powder

1 teaspoon xanthan gum

1 teaspoon salt

1 egg, beaten

125 ml/½ cup set plain yogurt

1 tablespoon ghee (clarified butter), melted and cooled, plus extra for brushing (optional)

scant 1 tablespoon black onion seeds

yellow cornflour/fine cornmeal, for dusting

2 large baking sheets, greased

Makes 6

The humble crumpet – so comforting spread with butter – is one of the things my friend Lucy misses most on her gluten-free diet. We have tried several store-bought versions but none of them are as nice as their wheat counterparts. This is our recipe, which is, in Lucy's view, a huge improvement on store-bought gluten-free crumpets.

crumpets

1 tablespoon caster/granulated sugar

1 tablespoon fast-action dried yeast

400 ml/1⅔ cups warm milk

300 ml/1¼ cups warm water

300 g/2⅓ cups gluten-free strong white bread flour

150 g/1 cup plus 2 tablespoons gluten-free plain/all-purpose flour

1 teaspoon baking powder

½ teaspoon bicarbonate of soda/ baking soda

½ teaspoon salt

1 teaspoon vanilla extract

butter, melted, for greasing

4 x 9-cm/3½-inch chefs' or crumpet rings

Makes 10–12

Put the sugar and yeast in a jug/pitcher with the warm milk and water. Leave for about 10 minutes in a warm place until a thick foam forms on top of the liquid.

Sift the flours, baking powder and bicarbonate of soda/baking soda into a large mixing bowl and whisk in the salt and vanilla along with the yeast mixture. Cover the bowl with clingfilm/plastic wrap and leave for 45 minutes in a warm place until the mixture has doubled in size.

Grease the chef's rings lightly with butter. Grease a frying pan or griddle with a little butter and set it over medium heat. Place the chefs' rings in the pan and pour a small ladleful of the crumpet batter into each ring. Cook for about 10 minutes until holes form on top of the crumpet, then remove the rings using oven gloves. Turn the crumpets over and cook for a further 5–10 minutes until the crumpet is golden brown and there is no scrunching noise when you press your finger down on top of the crumpet. When cooked, remove the crumpets from the pan or griddle and repeat the process until all the batter is used.

The crumpets are best served warm so eat them straight away, or if you are serving later that day, toast them to reheat before serving. They freeze well and can be toasted from frozen.

Brioche does take a long time to make but one slice of this buttery bread and you will realise that it is definitely worth the effort. The dough will be quite sticky before the first proving, but don't worry as it will become more manageable and easy to handle after proving.

brioche

Put the warm water in a jug/pitcher with the yeast and 1 tablespoon of the sugar and leave in a warm place for about 10 minutes until a thick foam has formed on top of the liquid.

Sift the flour and xanthan gum into the bowl of the stand mixer and add the remaining sugar. Pour in the yeast liquid and mix with a dough hook for 2–3 minutes. With the mixer running, beat in the eggs one at a time until you have a smooth dough. Once all the eggs are added, mix the dough for a further 3 or so minutes until it is smooth and silky.

Add the butter, cube by cube, to the dough whilst still mixing, until all the butter is incorporated and the dough is glossy and comes away from the sides of the bowl. The dough will be quite sticky. Cover the bowl with lightly greased clingfilm/plastic wrap and leave to prove in a warm place for about 3 hours until the dough has doubled in size. Knock back the dough on a flour-dusted surface and knead again with your hands, dusting liberally with flour.

Divide the dough in half, shape into two balls and place one in each of the prepared brioche pans. Whisk together the egg and sugar for the glaze and brush over the dough with a pastry brush (you may not need it all). Cover each loaf lightly with a layer of clingfilm/plastic wrap and leave in a warm place for 1–2 hours until the loaves have doubled in size again.

Preheat the oven to 180°C (350°F) Gas 4 and bake the brioche for 25–30 minutes until they are golden brown and sound hollow when you tap them.

The brioche is best eaten warm from the oven spread with butter and preserves.

For the brioche

60 ml/¼ cup warm water

7 g/1 envelope fast-action dried yeast

70 g/⅓ cup caster/granulated sugar

500 g/4 cups gluten-free strong white bread flour, plus extra for or dusting

1 teaspoon xanthan gum

7 eggs

375 g/3 sticks plus 2 tablespoons butter, slightly softened and cubed

For the glaze

1 egg

2 tablespoons caster/granulated sugar

a stand mixer fitted with a dough hook

2 brioche pans, about 16 cm/ 6 inches diameter, greased

Makes 2 loaves

These doughnuts are an extra-special treat and the variations are endless too! Pop a square of chocolate in the middle of each doughnut when shaping, or add the grated zest of two lemons to the dough and fill with lemon curd for a tangy treat.

cinnamon maple doughnuts

2 teaspoons fast-action dried
  yeast
100 ml/⅓ cup warm water
90 g/scant ½ cup caster/
  granulated sugar
350 g gluten-free self raising flour
  OR 2½ cups plus 1 tablespoon
  gluten-free all-purpose baking
  flour plus 2 teaspoons baking
  powder and 1 teaspoon
  xanthan gum
a pinch of fine sea salt
200 g/2 cups ground almonds
60 g/½ stick butter, chilled
  and cubed
1 egg
1 tablespoon maple syrup
2 teaspoons ground cinnamon
1½ tablespoons sour cream
about 1 litre/4 cups vegetable oil
caster/superfine sugar mixed with
  ground cinnamon, for dusting
about 300 g/1 cup plum preserve
  (optional)

a baking sheet, greased
a piping bag, fitted with a jam/
jelly nozzle/tip (optional)

Makes 20 doughnuts

Put the yeast, warm water and 1 tablespoon of the sugar in a small bowl and leave in a warm place for 5–10 minutes, until a foam forms on top.

Sift the flour into a mixing bowl, add the salt and ground almonds and rub in the butter with your fingertips. Add the egg, maple syrup, cinnamon, sour cream and yeast mixture and mix with your hands. Knead gently to form a soft, pliable dough – adding a little flour if the mixture is too sticky.

Divide the mixture into 20 balls of equal size. Put them on the prepared baking sheet, cover with oiled clingfilm/plastic wrap and leave in a warm place for about 1 hour, until the doughnuts have increased in size.

Heat the oil in a large saucepan – you will need sufficient oil to allow the doughnuts to float slightly above the base to ensure even cooking. To test whether the oil is hot enough, add a scrap of the dough to the pan – if it sizzles, floats to the top and turns golden brown the oil is ready. Cook the doughnuts in small batches for about 3–5 minutes on each side, until they are golden brown.

Mix the caster/superfine sugar and cinnamon together on a plate and position it near to your saucepan. Remove the cooked doughnuts from the pan with a slotted spoon, drain on paper towels and roll in the cinnamon sugar. Leave to cool on a sheet of baking parchment.

If you are filling the doughnuts, pass the preserve through a fine-meshed sieve/strainer to remove any lumps, then spoon into the piping bag. Make a cavity in each doughnut, using a teaspoon handle and wiggling it around. Squeeze a little plum preserve into each doughnut. This is easiest done whilst the doughnuts are still warm (but not hot), taking care that you don't overfill.

These doughnuts are best eaten on the day they are made.

Stollen is a deliciously rich and buttery fruit bread, which is said to have originated in 14th-century Germany. Traditionally stollen are cooked in special pans, which give the loaves their classic shape, but if you haven't got a stollen pan you can just shape the dough into a loaf on the baking sheet with your hands.

spiced stollen

Preheat the oven to 180°C (350°F) Gas 4.

Sift the flour and baking powder into a mixing bowl. Add the eggs with 3½ tablespoons of the melted butter, sour cream and sugar. Stir in the vanilla extract, pistachios, pecans, orange zest, spices, marzipan, sultanas/golden raisins and raisins. Spoon the batter into the prepared pan and then invert onto a baking sheet so that the dough is covered by the pan. If you do not have a stollen pan, shape the dough into a long oval loaf, about 35 x 20 cm/14 x 8 inches, dusting your hands with flour as you work.

Bake in the preheated oven for 40–50 minutes, until the top of the stollen is golden, gently lifting away the pan (if using) to see if it is cooked. Brush the cooked loaf with the remaining melted butter and dust with icing/confectioners' sugar, which will be absorbed by the butter to give the loaf a sugary coating.

This stollen will keep for up to 5 days if stored in an airtight container.

250 g gluten-free self-raising flour plus 3 teaspoons baking powder OR 2 scant cups gluten-free all-purpose baking flour plus 5 teaspoons baking powder and 1 teaspoon xanthan gum

3 eggs, beaten

75 g/5 tablespoons butter, melted and cooled

285 ml/1 cup plus 2½ tablespoons sour cream

100 g/¾ cup plus 1 tablespoon caster/granulated sugar

1 teaspoon vanilla extract

50 g/½ cup pistachios, chopped

50 g/½ cup pecans, chopped

grated zest of 1 large orange

2 teaspoons ground cinnamon

1 teaspoon mixed spice/apple pie spice

200 g/⅔ cup marzipan, cut into small pieces

80 g/½ cup sultanas/golden raisins

80 g/½ cup raisins

icing/confectioners' sugar, for dusting

a 38 x 13-cm/15 x 5-inch stollen pan, greased and lined

Makes 1 large loaf

desserts

I have yet to meet a person who doesn't enjoy profiteroles. These light choux buns are filled with cream and crushed fresh raspberries and are served drizzled with a rich chocolate sauce – delicious! I've found that choux pastry works extremely well with gluten-free flour and your guests won't be able to tell the difference.

raspberry & chocolate profiteroles

Preheat the oven to 200°C (400°F) Gas 6.

To make the choux buns, sift the flour twice to remove any lumps. Heat the butter in a saucepan with 150 ml/²⁄₃ cup cold water, until the butter is melted. Bring to the boil, then remove from the heat and shoot in the flour all in one go (very quickly). Beat hard with a wooden spoon until the dough forms a ball and no longer sticks to the sides of the pan. Leave to cool for about 5 minutes. Add the vanilla egg mixture a small amount at a time and use a wooden spoon to beat them into the dough. The mixture will form a sticky paste which holds its shape when you lift the whisk up. Spoon into the piping bag and pipe 20 balls of dough onto the prepared baking sheets. With clean hands, wet your finger and smooth down any peaks so that the pastry is smooth. Bake in the preheated oven for 12 minutes, then use a sharp knife to puncture each bun to allow the steam to escape. Return them to the oven for a further 2–5 minutes, until crisp. Cool on a wire rack and then cut in half.

Whip the cream to stiff peaks, fold in the raspberries and icing/confectioners' sugar and use to fill the profiteroles.

To make the chocolate sauce, put all the ingredients in a saucepan and heat, stirring, until melted. Serve the profiteroles immediately, with the warm sauce spooned over the top.

These profiteroles are best eaten on the day they are made as they contain fresh cream.

For the choux pastry
65 g/½ cup gluten-free plain/
   all-purpose baking flour
50 g/3½ tablespoons butter
2 large eggs, beaten with
   2 teaspoons vanilla extract

For the filling
250 ml/1 cup double/heavy cream
150 g/1 cup raspberries
1 generous tablespoon icing/
   confectioners' sugar, sifted

For the chocolate sauce
50 g/2 oz dark chocolate
50 ml/scant ¼ cup double/heavy
   cream
1 tablespoon golden/light corn
   syrup
1 tablespoon butter

*a piping bag fitted with a large
round nozzle/tip*
2 baking sheets, greased and lined

Makes 20 profiteroles

These delicate light pastries, filled with dessert wine and honey-poached nectarines are a real treat in summer when the fruits are in season. You can substitute peaches or apricots in place of the nectarines if you prefer.

nectarine & cream choux rings

1 quantity Choux Pastry dough
   (see page 168)
50 g/½ cup flaked/sliced almonds
3 ripe nectarines, pitted and
   thickly sliced
125 ml/½ cup sweet dessert wine
1 tablespoon honey
1 teaspoon vanilla extract
250 ml/1 cup double/heavy
   cream
1 generous tablespoon icing/
   confectioners' sugar, plus extra
   for dusting

*2 piping bags, 1 fitted with a large
round nozzle and the other fitted
with a large star nozzle/tip*
a baking sheet, greased and lined

Makes 12 rings

Preheat the oven to 200°C (400°F) Gas 6.

Spoon the choux pastry dough into the piping bag fitted with a round nozzle/tip and pipe 12 rings of choux pastry onto the prepared baking sheet. With clean hands wet your finger and smooth down any peaks from the piping so that the pastry is smooth. Sprinkle with flaked/sliced almonds.

Bake in the preheated oven for 15 minutes, then use a sharp knife to puncture each ring to allow the steam to escape. Return them to the oven for a further 5 minutes, until crisp. Cool on a wire rack and then cut in half.

Put the nectarines in a saucepan with the wine, honey and vanilla extract. Simmer over gentle heat for 5 minutes. Leave to cool completely.

Whip the cream to stiff peaks, sift in the icing/confectioners' sugar and whisk in. Spoon the cream into the piping bag fitted with a star nozzle/tip and pipe a ring of cream onto the base of each choux ring.

Drain the poached nectarines and cut into small pieces with a sharp knife. Arrange a few on top of the cream. Top with the remaining choux halves and dust with icing/confectioners' sugar. Serve immediately or cover and refrigerate until needed.

These choux rings are best eaten on the day they are made as they contain fresh cream.

Pecan pie is the classic American dessert. This recipe has crunchy pecan nuts enrobed in rich buttery caramel with hints of cinnamon and vanilla, all encased in a cream cheese pastry. Serve warm or cold with cream.

toffee pecan tart

To make the pastry, sift the flour into a mixing bowl and stir in the ground almonds. Rub in the butter until the mixture resembles fine breadcrumbs. Add the cream cheese, sugar, egg yolk and vanilla extract and use your fingers to mix together to a soft dough, adding a little cold water if the mixture is too dry. Wrap in clingfilm/plastic wrap and chill in the fridge for 1 hour.

Preheat the oven to 180°C (350°F) Gas 4. Put both the sugars, cinnamon, vanilla extract, butter, and both syrups in a saucepan and gently heat until the sugar has dissolved and the butter melted. Remove the pan from the heat and let the mixture cool for 10 minutes before beating in the eggs. Strain the syrup mixture into a measuring jug/pitcher – you should have about 600 ml/2⅓ cups of toffee syrup.

Bring the pastry to room temperature and break it into small pieces. Put the pieces in the prepared tin/pan and press out evenly with your fingertips, until the base is covered with a thin layer of pastry and there are no gaps. Trim away any excess pastry from around the top edge of the tin/pan. Fill the pastry case with the pecans and pour over 500 ml/2 cups of the syrup mixture so that the nuts are covered and the pastry case almost full. Bake in the preheated oven for 20–30 minutes, until the filling is set and the pastry golden brown. Gently reheat the remaining syrup and brush over the top of the tart whilst it is still warm using a pastry brush.

This tart will keep for up to 3 days if stored in an airtight container.

150 g/¾ cup caster/granulated sugar

150 g/⅔ cup dark soft brown sugar

2 generous teaspoons ground cinnamon

2 teaspoons vanilla extract

100 g/7 tablespoons butter

5 generous tablespoons golden/ light corn syrup

60 ml/scant ¼ cup maple syrup

3 eggs

300 g/3 cups pecans, finely chopped

For the pastry

250 g/2 cups gluten-free plain/ all-purpose baking flour

50 g/½ cup ground almonds

100 g/7 tablespoons butter, chilled

100 g/½ cup cream cheese

50 g/¼ cup caster/granulated sugar

1 egg yolk

1 teaspoon vanilla extract

a 23-cm/9-inch loose-based flan tin/pan, greased and lined

Makes 12 slices

When my friend Lucy was diagnosed with wheat intolerance, her partner David adapted his mum's family apple pie recipe to be gluten-free and very kindly shared his recipe with me. It is always popular and whenever served, every last crumb disappears. It is best served warm with crème fraîche or Greek yogurt.

David's apple streusel pie

3 large cooking apples, peeled and cored

caster/granulated sugar, too taste

175 g/1¾ cups ground almonds

175 g/¾ cup dark soft brown sugar

1 generous teaspoon ground cinnamon

175 g/1 stick plus 4 tablespoons unsalted butter, cubed

For the pastry

115 g/¾ cup plus 1 tablespoon gluten-free plain/all-purpose baking flour

115 g/scant 1 cup almond flour

50 g/⅓ cup icing/confectioners' sugar

115 g/1 stick butter, chilled and cubed

2 egg yolks

a 23-cm/9-inch loose-based, deep fluted tart tin/pan, greased

baking beans

Serves 10

To make the pastry, sift the flours and icing/confectioners' sugar into a mixing bowl. Rub the butter in with your fingertips or blitz in a food processor. Add the egg yolks and bring the dough together with your hands, adding a little water if necessary or extra flour if the dough is too soft. Wrap in clingfilm/plastic wrap and chill for at least 1 hour.

Preheat the oven to 180°C (350°F) Gas 4. Coarsely grate the chilled pastry into the prepared tart tin/pan and press it out with your thumbs, until the sides and base of the tin are covered with the pastry and there are no gaps. Prick the base with a fork and put in the freezer for 30 minutes. Line with baking parchment, fill with baking beans and bake in the preheated oven for 10–15 minutes.

Thinly slice the apples and put them in a saucepan with 1–2 tablespoons cold water. Cover with a tight-fitting lid and stew until very soft. Sweeten to taste with sugar, let cool slightly and then spoon into the blind-baked pastry case.

To make the topping, put the ground almonds, brown sugar and cinnamon in a food processor and blitz. Add the butter and blitz again to a paste. Take small balls of the mixture, press them between your finger and thumb to flatten and arrange them in an overlapping tiled pattern on top of the apple layer. Bake in the preheated oven for 40–50 minutes, until the topping is brown but still soft to the touch. Let cool slightly before serving.

This pie will keep for up to 5 days if refrigerated in an airtight container.

These dainty tartlets are the height of sophistication – crisp buttery pastry filled with real vanilla crème pâtissière and topped with glazed strawberries – they are the perfect accompaniment to a glass of chilled Prosecco at a summer garden party.

strawberry tartlets

To make the pastry, sift the flour into a mixing bowl and stir in the ground almonds. Rub in the butter until the mixture resembles fine breadcrumbs. Add the cream cheese, sugar, egg yolk, vanilla extract and lemon zest and mix to a soft dough with your fingers, adding a little water if the dough is too dry or extra flour if it is too sticky. Wrap in clingfilm/plastic wrap and chill for 1 hour.

Preheat the oven to 180°C (350°F) Gas 4. Dust a work surface with flour and use a rolling pin to roll out the pastry to a thickness of 3 mm/⅛ inch. Stamp out 24 rounds with the cutter and press one into each hole of the prepared tin/pan. Line the pastry cases with baking parchment, fill with baking beans and bake in the preheated oven for 12–15 minutes, until golden brown and crisp. Let cool on a wire rack.

To make the crème pâtissèrie, put the cornflour/cornstarch, sugar, egg and egg yolk in a bowl and whisk until creamy. Put the milk, cream and vanilla pod/bean in a saucepan and bring to the boil. Pour the hot milk over the egg mixture, whisking continuously. Return to the pan and cook for about 2 minutes, until thick. Remove the vanilla pod, pass the mixture through a sieve/strainer and let cool. Spoon the cooled crème pâtissière into the piping bag and fill the pastry cases. Arrange some strawberry halves on top. Put the preserve and lemon juice in a saucepan and heat until runny, pass through a sieve/strainer, let cool slightly, then brush over the top of each tartlet to glaze using a pastry brush.

These tartlets are best eaten on the day they are made.

1 tablespoon cornflour/cornstarch
60 g/scant ⅓ cup caster/granulated sugar
1 egg plus 1 egg yolk
100 ml/⅓ cup milk
150 ml/⅔ cup double/heavy cream
1 vanilla pod/bean, split lengthwise
300 g/1½ cups strawberries, hulled and halved
5 tablespoons apricot preserve
freshly squeezed juice of 2 small lemons

For the pastry
250 g/2 scant cups gluten-free plain/all-purpose baking flour plus 1 teaspoon xanthan gum
50 g/½ cup plus 3 tablespoons ground almonds
100 g/7 tablespoons butter, chilled
100 g/½ cup cream cheese
50 g/¼ cup caster/granulated sugar
1 egg yolk
1 teaspoon vanilla extract
grated zest of 1 lemon

an 8-cm/3-inch cutter
2 x 12-hole mini tartlet tins/pans, greased with butter
baking beans
a piping bag, fitted with a large round nozzle/tip

Makes 24 tartlets

If there is one recipe that I've wrestled with for a long time it was this one! I knew it was going to be difficult, but even I was surprised when my attempts were more 'brick-like' than delicate leaves of millefeuille pastry. After weeks of trying I finally found a recipe that worked – more by chance than by any scientific process. It is not made in the same way as traditional puff pastry so the process may seem a little strange but it is the best method I have found for thin leaves of pastry and I'm delighted to be able to share it with you here.

blackcurrant & vanilla slices

300 ml/1¼ cups double/heavy
   cream, whipped
4 generous tablespoons
   blackcurrant preserve
icing/confectioners' sugar,
   for dusting

Puff pastry
200 g/1¾ sticks butter, chilled
175 g/1⅓ cups plus 1 tablespoon
   gluten-free plain/all-purpose
   baking flour sifted, plus extra
   for dusting
1 teaspoon xanthan gum
2 teaspoons freshly squeezed
   orange juice
1 teaspoon almond extract
80–100 ml/¼–⅓ cup cold water

2 large baking sheets, greased
a piping bag fitted, with a large
star nozzle/tip

Makes 8 slices
(about 400 g/14 oz
puff pastry dough)

Cut half of the butter into small cubes and mix into the flour using a free-standing mixer or whisk. Add 80–100 ml/¼–⅓ cup cold water, together with the xanthan gum, orange juice and almond extract. You may not need all the water so add gradually. Mix until you have a soft (but not sticky) dough.

Coarsely grate the remaining butter and keep it chilled until required. Lay a large piece of baking parchment on a clean work surface and dust liberally with flour. Using a flour-dusted rolling pin, roll out the pastry to a 50 x 18-cm/20 x 7-inch rectangle. Sprinkle half of the grated butter over the pastry and dust liberally with flour. Fold one of the short ends of the pastry up into the middle of the pastry at third intervals. Next take the other thin end of the pastry and fold that down over the already folded pastry so that your pastry is folded into about a third of the size that it was originally and you have a 20 x 18-cm/8 x 7-inch rectangle. Dust the surface and rolling pin with more flour, turn the pastry over and roll out into a 50 x 18-cm/20 x 7-inch rectangle again, with the folds in the same direction as they were originally rolled (and not rotated as you would with traditional puff pastry). Sprinkle the rolled out pastry with the remaining grated butter, dust again with flour and repeat the folding steps. Dust the surface and rolling pin again and repeat the rolling out stages twice more (without adding any butter but still dusting with flour), each time ensuring that the folds and the direction you are rolling out are the same. This helps to ensure that the layers rise. For best results, use the pastry straightaway.

Preheat the oven to 180°C (350°F) Gas 4. Trim any rough edges and then cut out 16 rectangles, each about 8 x 5 cm/3¼ x 2 inch and 2.5–5 mm/⅛–¼ inch thickness. It is important to use a downward cutting motion with the knife rather than dragging it through the pastry as this may compress the pastry leaves, resulting in less rising of the pastry. Transfer to the baking sheets. Bake in the preheated oven for 10–15 minutes, until the pastry is golden brown and risen. Let cool on a wire rack. Spread 8 of the slices with a few spoonfuls of preserve. Spoon the cream into the piping bag and pipe large stars on top of the cream. Dust with icing/confectioners' sugar and serve immediately or refrigerate until needed. These slices are best eaten on the day they are made as they contain fresh cream.

I love cheesecake of all types but best of all is a plain baked vanilla cheesecake. This version, based loosely on the classic New York cheesecake, is delicious served with fresh berries. The recipe contains oats, which are not always suitable for all those with a gluten intolerance, but gluten-free oats are available so do use these. Alternatively, omit the base altogether and replace the oats with toasted coconut or make a simple crumb base using any gluten-free cookies and melted butter.

baked vanilla cheesecake

Preheat the oven to 160°C (325°F) Gas 3.

To make the base, put the butter and syrup in a large saucepan and melt over low heat. Stir in the oats and sugar, mixing well to ensure that all the oats are coated. Transfer the mixture to the prepared tin/pan and use the back of a spoon to press it down.

Put the eggs, cream cheese, 100 ml/⅓ cup of the sour cream, sugar, clotted/heavy cream and seeds from the vanilla pod/bean in a mixing bowl and whisk to combine.

Pour the mixture into the tin/pan on top of the base. Bake in the preheated oven for 1–1¼ hours, until the cheesecake is set but still wobbles slightly. Put the remaining sour cream and icing/confectioners' sugar in a bowl and whisk together. Remove the cheesecake from the oven and pour the sour cream mixture over the top. Return it to the oven and bake for a further 10 minutes. Let the cheesecake cool completely in the tin/pan then chill in the fridge before cutting into slices to serve.

This cheesecake will keep for up to 3 days if refrigerated in an airtight container.

For the base
100 g/7 tablespoons butter
5 tablespoons golden/light corn syrup
250 g/1½ cups gluten-free porridge/rolled oats
60 g/⅓ cup caster/granulated sugar

For the cheesecake
4 eggs
600 g/2½ cups cream cheese
400 ml/1⅓ cups sour cream
140 g/scant ¾ cup caster/granulated sugar
225 g/1 cup clotted or extra thick double/heavy cream
1 vanilla pod/bean, split
2 tablespoons icing/confectioners' sugar

a 20-cm/8-inch springform tin/pan, greased and lined

Serves 10

This rich chocolate torte, delicately perfumed with ground pistachios, is a perfect dessert to serve at a dinner party as it can be prepared in advance. To make it extra special why not serve the homemade pistachio ice cream on the side, for the ultimate pistachio treat.

chocolate torte with pistachio ice cream

For the torte

260 g/9½ oz dark chocolate

100 g/7 tablespoons butter

200 g/1½ cups icing/
confectioners' sugar, plus
extra for dusting

4 eggs, separated

1 teaspoon vanilla extract

100 g/1 scant cup shelled
pistachios, finely ground

For the pistachio ice cream

3 egg yolks

90 g/5 tablespoons caster/
granulated sugar

100 ml/⅓ cup milk

200 ml/¾ cup double/heavy
cream

100 g/scant 1 cup shelled
pistachios, finely chopped

½ teaspoon vanilla extract

green food colouring (optional)

*a 23-cm/9-inch springform cake
tin/pan, greased and lined*

an ice cream maker

Serves 8–10

Preheat the oven to 180°C (350°F) Gas 4.

To make the torte, put the chocolate in a heatproof bowl set over a pan of barely simmering water. Add the butter and melt, stirring occasionally. Remove the bowl from the heat and let cool.

Sift the icing/confectioners' sugar into a mixing bowl and add the egg yolks. Whisk until light, creamy and doubled in size. Fold in the melted chocolate mixture, vanilla extract and ground pistachios. Put the egg whites in a greasefree bowl and whisk until softly peaking. Gently fold the egg whites into the chocolate mixture, making sure everything is incorporated. Pour the batter into the prepared cake tin/pan. Bake in the preheated oven for 25–30 minutes, until a crust has formed on the top of the cake but it is still slightly soft underneath. It will set as it cools so let the cake cool completely in the tin/pan before removing it.

To make the ice cream, whisk together the egg yolks and sugar until thick and creamy. Put the milk, cream and pistachios in a saucepan and bring to the boil. Pour the hot milk and cream over the eggs, whisk together, then return to the pan and cook for a few minutes, until thickened. Add the vanilla extract and a few drops of green food colouring (if using). Let cool, then churn in an ice cream maker until frozen, following the manufacturer's instructions.

Dust the cooled torte with icing/confectioners' sugar and cut into slices. Serve with a scoop of ice cream on the side.

This torte will keep for up to 3 days if stored in an airtight container.

Crumble is the ultimate in comfort food desserts – here tangy plums with a hint of almond and vanilla, are buried beneath a buttery, melt-in-the-mouth crumble.

plum & amaretto crumble

Preheat the oven to 180°C (350°F) Gas 4.

Put the plums in a large saucepan. Split the vanilla pod/bean in half lengthwise with a sharp knife and use the tip of the knife to scrape the seeds directly into the saucepan. Add the vanilla pod/bean, sugar and amaretto. Simmer the plums over gentle heat for about 5 minutes, until softened. Remove and discard the vanilla pod/bean and transfer the fruit to the prepared baking dish.

To make the crumble topping, put the ground almonds in a mixing bowl and rub in the butter. Stir in the oats and sugar. Sprinkle the mixture over the plums and bake in the preheated oven for 35–40 minutes, until the topping is golden brown and the plum juices are bubbling around the edge of the dish. Serve warm or cold with cream.

This crumble is best eaten on the day it is made but can be refrigerated for up to 2 days.

800 g/1¾ lbs ripe red plums, halved and pitted
1 vanilla pod/bean
85 g/⅓ cup plus 2 tablespoons caster/granulated sugar
100 ml/⅓ cup amaretto or other almond-flavoured liquor

For the crumble topping
115 g/1 cup ground almonds
115 g/1 stick butter, chilled and cubed
115 g/⅔ cup gluten-free porridge/rolled oats
60 g/⅓ cup caster/granulated sugar

a large ovenproof baking dish, buttered

Serves 8

184

Delicate friand cakes, made extra light with whisked egg whites, are perfect served with warm griddled pineapple, flambéed in coconut rum and topped with a refreshing scoop of coconut ice cream.

friands with flambéed pineapple & coconut cream

60 g/⅔ cup desiccated coconut

115 g/1 stick butter, softened

115 g/½ cup plus 1 tablespoon
   caster/granulated sugar

2 large eggs, separated

60 g/½ cup ground almonds

2 tablespoons coconut rum

2 canned pineapple rings,
   finely chopped

1 teaspoon vanilla extract

For the coconut ice cream

3 egg yolks

150 g/¾ cup caster/granulated
   sugar

400 ml/1⅓ cups coconut milk

250 ml/1 cup double/heavy cream

60 ml/¼ cup coconut rum

For the flambéed pineapple

1 small pineapple, peeled and cut
   into wedges

1 tablespoon dark soft brown
   sugar

100 ml/⅓ cup coconut rum

*a 12-hole cupcake tin/pan,
greased with butter*

an ice cream maker

Makes 12 friands

Preheat the oven to 180°C (350°F) Gas 4.

To make the friands, put the coconut in a food processor and blitz until very finely ground. Put the butter, sugar and egg yolks in a mixing bowl and beat together until light and creamy. Whisk in the coconut and ground almonds, coconut rum, pineapple and vanilla extract. Put the egg whites in a separate greasefree bowl and whisk until stiffly peaking. Fold them into the cake batter, adding a third of the egg whites to loosen the mixture and then folding in the remainder. Divide the batter between the holes in the prepared tin/pan and bake in the preheated oven for 20–25 minutes, until the friands are golden brown. Let cool in the tin/pan.

To make the ice cream, put the egg yolks and sugar in a mixing bowl and whisk until thick and creamy. Put the coconut milk and cream in a saucepan and bring to the boil. Pour over the egg mixture, whisking continuously. Add the coconut rum and return the mixture to the pan and cook for 2–3 minutes, until the mixture starts to thicken. Let cool, then churn in an ice cream maker until frozen, following the manufacturer's instructions.

Heat a griddle pan until very hot. Cook the pineapple wedges for 2–3 minutes on each side, sprinkling with the brown sugar when you turn them. Pour over the rum – if you are cooking on a gas flame, take care as the rum will flambé. Serve the friands with some griddled pineapple and a scoop of coconut ice cream on the side. Serve immediately.

The coconut friands will keep for up to 2 days if stored in an airtight container.

Caramel, cinnamon and baked bananas – this is one of the most comforting desserts there is. Served with fresh whipped cream, enhanced with tropical coconut rum, this cake is a warm hug on a plate!

banana cake with rum cream

To prepare the caramel, put 100 g/½ cup of the caster/granulated sugar and 75 g/ 5 tablespoons of the butter in the tarte tatin pan and warm over direct heat, until the caramel turns golden brown. If using a springform tin/pan melt the sugar and butter in a saucepan until golden brown, then pour the caramel into the prepared pan. Peel the bananas and cut the bananas into 1 cm/½ in rounds and carefully place in rings in the warm caramel. Squeeze over the lemon juice to prevent the bananas from discolouring. Set aside whilst you prepare the polenta cake.

Preheat the oven to 180°C (350°F) Gas 4. Simmer the polenta in the 500 ml/ 2 cups water for about 5 minutes, until thick then leave to cool. Put the remaining butter and caster/granulated sugar and brown sugar in a mixing bowl and whisk until light and creamy. Beat in the eggs and whisk again. Add the ground pecans, cooked polenta, vanilla extract and cinnamon and whisk together well. Pour the cake batter over the bananas in caramel and bake in the preheated oven for about 1 hour, until the cake is set. If the cake starts to brown too much, cover loosely with a sheet of foil. Let cool in the pan for a few minutes, then invert the cake onto a plate so that the caramelized bananas are on the top. Take care as warm caramel may spill.

To make the rum cream, put the cream, icing/confectioners' sugar and rum in a mixing bowl and whisk to soft peaks. Serve the cake warm with spoonfuls of the rum cream on the side.

This cake will keep for up to 2 days if stored in an airtight container.

215 g/1 cup plus 1 tablespoon caster/granulated sugar
300 g/2 sticks plus 4½ tablespoons butter, softened
4 ripe bananas
freshly squeezed juice of 1 lemon
120 g/⅔ cup plus 1 tablespoon dried polenta
115 g/½ cup dark soft brown sugar
3 large eggs
120 g/1 cup shelled pecans, finely ground
1 teaspoon vanilla extract
1 generous teaspoon ground cinnamon

For the rum cream
300 ml/1¼ cups double/heavy cream
1 generous tablespoon icing/ confectioner's sugar, sifted
60 ml/¼ cup coconut rum

a 25-cm/10-inch cast-iron tarte tatin pan or springform cake tin/pan

Serves 8–10

index